Explaining
Intercession

Johannes Facius

Sovereign World

Bible quotations are taken from the NKJV New King James BIble.
© Copyright Thomas Nelson Publishers Inc.,
P.O. Box 141000, Nashville, TN 37214, USA.

ISBN: 1 85240 120 6

SOVEREIGN WORLD LIMITED
P.O. Box 777, Tonbridge, Kent TN11 9XT, England.

Typeset and printed in the UK by Sussex Litho Ltd, Chichester, West Sussex.

What Intercession Really Is

When asked about intercession many believers would say that it is prayer. But if that were the case it is strange that the word "intercession" is mentioned separately from the word "prayer". An example is found in 1 Timothy 2 where Paul mentions *"supplications, prayers, intercessions and giving of thanks"* as four different disciplines of the exercise of prayer. This gives us reason to believe that there therefore is a difference between prayer and intercession. However, let us try first of all to define what "intercession" really is.

The English word "intercession" might actually in itself give us a good idea about the meaning of intercession. The word means "to go in between". It describes how someone deliberately goes in between two parties to intervene in a situation of conflict and to try to keep the parties apart from one another. Also, it is interesting to notice how the word "prayer" is not directly implied in the word "intercession", from which we might also conclude that this is something different and implies more than ordinary prayer.

First of all, intercession is a position we take before God in a particular situation and for a specific cause, and not just something we can do for a couple of hours at a certain time. When people say that they were at the church to do intercession for two hours on Wednesday evening, they are in fact meaning that they were at the church and prayed for a couple of hours. Intercession cannot be practised for a couple of hours. It is an on-going commitment to remain in a position before God until the case has been solved. Intercession is in other words a twenty-four hour position, which means that the intercessor is before God in a very conscious way constantly, even if he is not able to actually pray for more than a small part of the time.

The power of such a position before God is very great. An example is Martin Luther. A few years ago, when my wife and I first moved to Germany, I made a trip to the city of Worms, where Luther in 1523 was put before the Catholic Church Council and the German Princes and was challenged to withdraw the 95 theses that he so boldly had nailed to the door of the Cathedral.

On a certain spot right in front of the Church there is a memorial stone in the ground which carries this inscription: "Here stood Martin Luther and he said: 'Here I stand and cannot but, so help me God.'" I was so deeply moved when I visited this place that I actually took off my shoes and placed myself on the stone, while crying out to God: "God make me into a man who can take a position and stick to it!" Martin Luther did intercession all those years ago, and his bold position did not only change his own life, it changed the world forever. God is looking for men and women who are willing to take up a position in the gap, so that He can work out His purposes on earth.

In the Bible, Moses is probably the clearest example of this. Moses did not just pray for the people of Israel when they were in great trouble because of their sins. He took up a position before God. Psalm 106:23 puts it this way,

"Therefore He [God] *said that He would destroy them, had not Moses His chosen one stood before Him in the breach to turn away His wrath, lest He destroy them."*

It is true that Moses pleaded in prayer with God to forgive the people, but the word "prayer" is not even mentioned here. It was not what Moses uttered with his mouth that had the greatest impact. It was the position he boldly took up before God that made the difference. From the record in the books of Moses, we know that Moses even dared get in the way of God when He was furious against Israel and wanted to burn them. The Lord actually said to Moses in a manner of speaking: "Get out of my way!" But Moses did not move one inch. And by this position he became like a wall of protection for the people against the wrath of the Lord.

When the Lord Jesus talked about *"praying without ceasing"*, He must have meant something like this. Surely He would not anticipate people being on their knees for 24 hours a day. Rather, He was talking about taking this conscious position in the spirit where you are before the Lord in a certain matter or for a certain

4

group of people even while you have to be about your daily work. The prophet Isaiah in the 62nd chapter, verses 6–7 speaks about the ministry of the watchman:

"I have set watchmen on your walls, O Jerusalem, Who shall never hold their peace day or night. You who make mention of the Lord, do not keep silent, And give Him no rest till He establishes And till He makes Jerusalem a praise in the earth."

Here we read about intercessors who don't just pray occasionally for Jerusalem, but who are in a firm position around the clock to remind the Lord about His promises. They are before the Lord "day and night" and give Him no rest.

Dr. Derek Prince explains in one of his books, that the word "watchman" in the Hebrew can be translated as "secretary", and he goes on outlining the specific characteristics of a secretary: she knows the agenda of her boss, and she keeps reminding her boss about his appointments. This is actually a very good picture of the work of an intercessor. We must know something about God's agenda and then keep on reminding Him to do what he promised to do in His word. We must learn to remain in a position before God until something happens concerning the issue for which we are praying. This is one of the clear characteristics of the work of intercession.

The second basic feature concerning the nature of intercession is that it always requires a sacrifice. When we are making ordinary prayer, we do not necessarily have to sacrifice anything except maybe some time during which we pray for a certain situation or for some friends of ours. We can sit in our safe position, in our secure place and we can pray for people distant from us who are in a situation of danger or great need.

I am not saying that this is not valid. All prayer is worthwhile and carries a reward in itself, but intercession is different from just praying for somebody else while you are still resting in your own secure place. Intercession requires sacrifice. And that sacrifice comes naturally because, if you want to intercede for somebody, you need to be able to identify with that person, and that will require something extra from you. You might not be able in a physical sense to enter into the shoes of the person you are interceding for, but you must be able by the help of the Holy Spirit to identify with them in the spiritual sense and take upon yourself the whole situation of that person for whom you are interceding. This is what we call the principle of identification. We will deal in more detail with this later. At this point, it is enough to say that intercession cannot be made without paying some kind of sacrifice.

When we look at the lives of the great intercessors in the Bible, we find this to be very true. First and foremost, we can look into the life of the greatest intercessor ever; namely the Lord Jesus Himself. Both in Romans 8:34 and Hebrews 7:25–27, it speaks about the Lord Jesus as always making intercession before the throne of God.

This is the ministry that the Lord Jesus has held since His death and resurrection and ascension into the heavenly throne-room where He is now sitting at the right-hand side of the Father. For almost two thousand years, the Lord Jesus has been our intercessor, the intercessor of the Church, the intercessor of the people of Israel, and the intercessor of the world. This is one fact that underlines the great importance and power within the ministry of intercession. The Lord Jesus had a ministry upon the earth for three and a half years, but He has now been holding up the ministry of intercession for nearly two thousand years.

Both Scripture references in Romans and Hebrews point out that it is not only because of the prayers of Jesus on our behalf that the Father is blessing us so much. It is more because of the sacrifice of Jesus when He gave His very own life for us, which is reflected in His intercession for us.

The sacrifice is the factor that gives intercession its tremendous power. The Lord Jesus could have been praying for us while remaining in heaven forever, feeling sorrow for our sins and appealing before His Father for forgiveness, but He chose to leave the glory and humble Himself and become a man; a man of suffering and a man of sorrows, and finally offering up His life on the cross to atone for our sins.

It is the sacrifice He made that is the background of the power of intercession of the Lord Jesus before the Father. The Father is ever reminded of the fact that when Jesus is praying for us, He was the one who first laid down His life for us and died for us, bearing all our sins. This is where intercession again differs from ordinary prayer. Intercession requires a sacrifice, and it is the sacrifice that impacts the heart of the Father.

You can imagine what impact it has on the Father's heart; how would He be able to refuse anything that the Lord Jesus requires in prayer from Him, while He is ever being reminded of that great sacrifice that His dear Son made on our behalf?

If we look at the life of the Apostle Paul, another great intercessor in the Bible, we find that the very same principle applies. In Romans 10:1 Paul is interceding for his fellow-citizens, the Jewish people, and he expresses that it is his heart's desire and prayer to God for Israel that they may be saved

"For I bear them witness that they have a zeal for God, but not according to knowledge."

And in the previous chapter 9, in the first verses, the heart of Paul is revealed concerning his relationship to the Jewish people. He says as follows (verses 1–3):

"I tell the truth in Christ, I am not lying, my conscience also bearing me witness in the Holy Spirit, that I have great sorrow and continual grief in my heart. For I could wish that I myself were accursed from Christ for my brethren, my kinsmen according to the flesh, who are Israelites."

This is one of the most remarkable statements by the Apostle Paul concerning his relationship to his fellow-citizens, the Jews. He is speaking about something that has been put into his heart by the Holy Spirit, a great sorrow and a continual grief, and then he brings this amazing statement that he could wish that he himself was accursed from Christ if it could serve any purpose for his countrymen, the Israelites. Here, Paul reveals the Spirit of the Lord Jesus Himself, being willing to die and even to be separated from God for eternity if that sacrifice could ever bring his fellow Jews to salvation. This is actually the very heart of Jesus that Paul is expressing.

Of course, the Lord could not accept this kind of offer because it really would not work out that way. Even if Paul were accursed from Christ, he could not save anybody by doing so. Only the death of the Lord Jesus, the Son of God, the sinless Lamb of God, is able to atone for the sins of people. So, God could never have accepted Paul's offer, but I am sure that it is true to say that the Lord must have been deeply impressed by that spirit expressed in the heart of the Apostle Paul and how he was willing not just to put down his life in the body, but even to be accursed from Christ in order to bring salvation to his brethren, the Israelites. It is that kind of spirit that gives intercession its tremendous power. And it is that testimony of the Apostle Paul in chapter 9 that underlines his desire in chapter 10 to pray that Israel may be saved. So, here we see the principle of intercession, which is to be willing to make sacrifices in order for other people to come to know the truth.

In a way, we are not even talking about a New Testament spirit in this area of intercession. We have already made reference to Moses, the great intercessor, whom the Lord used to lead His people of Israel out of Egypt to the Promised Land. Four times during the journey throughout the wilderness, God became so upset with His own people because of their rebellion and their sins that He wanted to punish them and even destroy them, but because of the intercession of Moses the people were rescued and were allowed to continue their journey.

Earlier in this chapter, we quoted from Psalm 106 about Moses, God's man, who stood in the breach to protect the Israelites from the wrath of God. We would have to understand that by doing so, Moses was really running a big risk.

We recall from Exodus 32, especially after the tragedy with the golden calf, how the wrath of God burned against the Israelites and that the Lord said to Moses that He would burn and destroy the people and then He would make another beginning with Moses, but how Moses then boldly took up this position in the gap and replied to the Lord that he would be willing for his name to be taken out of the Book of Life if God would only spare the people. Moses was also in his heart prepared to pay an enormous sacrifice for the people of Israel to be saved from the wrath of God.

Furthermore, Moses risked his physical life by standing up to God in that situation as he could not possibly know if God would actually carry out this threat, which would have meant that Moses would have been the first one to be slain by the fire of God.

So, we see that in real intercession, there is a risk, and a sacrifice connected. The heart of God was so deeply moved by Moses' intercession and his willingness to sacrifice both his physical life and his eternity on behalf of this rebellious people of God that God forgave the people because of Moses' prayer. However, it wasn't the prayer that saved the people, it was the sacrifice. It was Moses' willingness, as it were, to step into the spirit of the cross, the spirit of laying down your life, the spirit of giving up your own for the benefit and the blessing of others. That is what made the difference and moved the heart of God to forgive this grave sin of idolatry and be willing to continue letting His people walk through the wilderness towards the Promised Land.

In the case of Moses, we also see that God was not willing to accept the great offer that he made. First of all, it is not for anybody to suggest his name to be removed from the Book of Life. This is God's own sovereign choice. Secondly, there was and there is no need for anybody to die for the sins of others, other than the only one who was appointed to do so; namely the Lord Jesus Christ.

In intercession, we cannot make these kinds of offers; we might have the same spirit and we might be willing to do so, but God would never accept these kinds of sacrifices because He already accepted one sacrifice for all; the sacrifice of His own dearly beloved Son, the Lord Jesus. So, this is not what we could expect or even what God would expect of us. But the spirit is important, and there are a lot of sacrifices that God would require and that we would be able to give in order to make our prayers heard and to call down an answer to them from heaven.

One very obvious sacrifice that goes along with prayer and intercession is fasting. Fasting is giving a bit of yourself. It is to a certain extent laying down something of your own life and your own self, which is an act that will always energize and empower our prayer life. That is why, in the New Testament, prayer is closely connected to fasting. Fasting in itself is not worth much more than the bodily benefit you can get from it, but when fasting is joined with prayer, it becomes a tremendous, powerful addition to our prayer life because it signifies a sacrifice given along with our intercession.

Sacrifices are important to God when He looks down and listens to the prayers of His people because they are evidence of a great determination to have the prayers heard. When people are willing to pay a price in order to be heard, the heart of God is impressed tremendously.

The power of fasting can even be seen in the world. We know in recent years that this evil idea of hunger-strikes or taking a hostage has been a very powerful instrument in the hands of people who were trying to obtain something from a government. When I was in Ireland a year ago, I heard about the hunger-strike of five young IRA men in the Maze prison, and how this, their sacrifice of starvation unto death, had turned them into great heroes among the IRA people, even to such a degree that it had reinforced the violence and the dedication of the people committed to the IRA cause.

We have also seen other examples of people who after being refused a request from a government went on a hunger-strike, perhaps in front of the parliament building with the media present, thus releasing tremendous power by practically twisting the arms of powerful governments to give them what they required. If this kind of hunger-striking principle or the one of hostage-taking is effective on the evil side of the fence, how much more powerful will it be when it is done in love before God to save people from judgement and catastrophes.

We see how important it is that we are willing to pay sacrifices. It is a part of the life of intercession. It is not only speaking about fasting in terms of abstaining from eating food, but also in the area of time. Do we really have time to give to God? This is an important sacrifice that we need to pay if we want to see the Lord move. We need to sacrifice other things and give time to seek His face for that which is so much upon our hearts.

This is probably an even more difficult thing for modern believers to do in our very busy-minded age. But if we are not willing to put aside other things that are taking up our time and come before the Lord and plead our cases before Him, we will never be able to see real breakthroughs in our prayer-life. Fasting from food is one way of paying a sacrifice; fasting from other time-consuming activities is another one that we need to make up our minds to bring.

There is one thing about the Lord that we might not understand, but which is quite true; the Lord does not seem to be in a hurry to respond to people's requests in prayer. It is as if the Lord Himself is taking His time to wait before answering the prayers of His saints. There could be many reasons why the Lord is doing this, and we might not even know the real one, but it would not be strange to suggest that one of the reasons why God is not quick to respond to anybody's prayers is that He desires to see whether we are really sincere and earnest about the things we are praying for. This is also why we need time when we come before God. It is said in the book of Exodus about Moses that the Lord called him up to the mountain and said to him, *"Stay here and wait for Me."* We understand from this that Moses was called to go up and wait for God maybe for a couple of days before the Lord called him into His presence.

The Lord is never apt to give quick answers. The Lord wants to see if we have a heart for Him, if we have determination, and if we really desire the things that we are praying for so much that we are willing to persevere before His face. This is another area of sacrifice when we talk about intercession. Ordinary prayers can be quickly prayed and quickly forgotten, and God might respond to some of them, but intercession is different. Intercession is a long-term battle; it is a testing time for our determination and our sincerity of heart before the Lord. Without sacrifices, intercession will never really be effective.

The Dynamics of Intercession

Let's talk about the factors that make intercession such a powerful ministry. In this connection, I actually dare make the statement that in my estimation, intercession is more powerful than all Christian ministries put together. I am of course not making that statement because I happen to be in that particular ministry, but because I believe there is biblical proof that intercession is a ministry that can accomplish things that no other Christian ministry could ever accomplish. To me, the Word of God presents clear evidence that intercession is the only ministry that can change the course of a nation.

There are two Old Testament scriptures that I would like to refer to in this connection. Firstly, Isaiah 59:16 where the prophet is saying the following, *"He* [that is, the Lord] *saw that there was no man, and wondered that there was no intercessor; Therefore, His own arm brought salvation for Him; And His own righteousness, it sustained Him."* This is a scripture that comes in chapter 59 where the overall subjects are the sins and the rebellion of the people of Israel, and the judgement of the Lord upon His people because of their sins. It is in this context that we have this surprising statement about the Lord; that when coming down to put judgement upon Israel, He saw that there was no man and He wondered that there was no intercessor.

In other words, the Lord had expected somebody to stand in the gap and come before Him and plead the people's case, but He was surprised and wondered that there was not one single man to be found. Therefore, the Lord took action on His own and went out in righteousness and justice to deal with His people.

Now, the amazing thought is that if a man had been there; if an intercessor had been found, it would have made a difference to the way the Lord would have dealt with His people. If that were not so and if God had already made up His mind that He would punish His people, why on earth would He be looking for an intercessor, or be surprised not to find one? Why would He be doing all this unless He means that had He found an intercessor there, He would have kept back His wrath and maybe found another way of solving the problem? Now, for the people of Israel this would have meant the severe punishment that God was putting upon His people could have been prevented.

Or to put it in another way; it means that intercession has the capacity to change the course of a nation. We need to understand that it does not say that when God came down to judge His people here, He had expected to see an evangelist there, or that He was surprised that there was no pastor, or that He would have been grateful if there had been a prophet or an apostle. No, the word is "intercessor". Evangelists are needed, pastors are needed as are prophets and apostles for the Kingdom of God in the Church today, but none of these ministries have in themselves the power to change the course of a whole nation. As far as we can see in the Word only intercession has the possibility of doing something about a national situation. This is why I believe intercession is so important.

You will also remember, of course, from way back in history what happened to Sodom and Gomorrah. How the Lord came down to see what was happening in these wicked cities and, how on His way down to investigate the situation, He stopped before Abraham. It was the Lord's initiative to stop and talk to Abraham about what He was about to do in Sodom and Gomorrah, and the indication is clearly that the Lord wanted Abraham to intercede for Sodom and Gomorrah, which he did. And it is of course true that the intercession of Abraham saved Lot and his family, or at least gave them the opportunity to get saved and to be taken out of Sodom and Gomorrah before the fire fell from heaven and destroyed the cities. But Genesis 18 indicates that there was much more in it than just the salvation of one man and his family.

In the intercession of Abraham the issue was not Lot and his family, but whether God would spare the whole place if enough righteous people could be found. It was not just a concern about his relatives that made Abraham intercede before God, but there was a desire in his heart to see God withhold His hand from destroying ten thousand inhabitants in the twin cities of Sodom and Gomorrah.

We see this clearly when Abraham begins his intercession and his negotiations with the Lord and he keeps challenging the Lord, saying, *"Lord, if you find fifty righteous people, will you then spare the place?"* and *"… if you find forty… thirty… twenty…"* The issue is not the salvation of Lot and his family. The issue is the salvation of the doomed cities. Abraham's last offer is ten righteous people, *"Lord, will you then spare the place?"* and the Lord agrees to these terms. However, as we know, there weren't even ten righteous people, and so in the end, Sodom and Gomorrah were destroyed.

Nevertheless, the interesting thing is that God's heart went out to find a possible solution because you see, our God is not interested in the death of any sinner. God took the initiative to call Abraham to stand in the gap and to intercede for Sodom and Gomorrah. Unfortunately, the terms of God for saving the cities could not be met. That is another matter. However, it does not take away the principle or the truth that intercession in a responsible – I would even say in the required manner – in any city, would have a possibility of influencing the heart of God to turn away the judgement that is coming, and bring revival and salvation to the people of that city.

Also, in Ezekiel 22:30, 31; we have the same amazing thought; *'"I sought for a man among them who would make a wall, and stand in the gap before Me on behalf of the land, that I should not destroy it; but I found no one. Therefore, I have poured out My indignation on them; I have consumed them with the fire of My wrath; and I have recompensed their deeds on their own heads," says the Lord God.'*

This is another amazing opportunity that unfortunately was lost. The picture is the same as the one in Isaiah 59; the people had fallen away from the Lord, sin had abounded, and the Lord had come to the point where He could no longer tolerate what was going on in the people of Israel. And so, He was moving towards His own people in judgement, and then all of a sudden comes this statement that *"God was seeking for a man who would make a wall; who would stand in the gap"*, and the Lord clearly says *"… that I would not destroy it…,"* but unfortunately the conclusion is this *"… but I found no one."*

Now, God would never joke about a serious situation like this, so we have every right to conclude that if a single man could have been found in this situation who would build a wall and stand in the gap between the Lord and the people in intercessory prayer, God would not have destroyed the land and there would have been found another way of dealing with the sins of the people. Because actually, God is able to deal with the sins of a nation in more than one way.

I am not saying that our intercession can prevent God from judging evil, or that because of intercession God would tolerate sin forever. This is not true. By intercession, we can never talk about changing the will of God, because His will cannot be changed. But we can talk about the way in which God would execute His will, and this is a different matter. What we are seeing here, is that it is possible for God in dealing with the sins of a city or a nation, to approach that sinful situation in a way other than simply destroying the land and the people.

Another way that God can destroy sin is through revival; through bringing people on their knees to repent before Him. We know that from the case of another city, namely the city of Nineveh, spoken of by the Prophet Jonah. This city was also faced with the severe judgement of God and was destined for destruction, but through the message of Jonah, the whole people repented, from the king in the castle, even to the cattle in the field, and they turned away from their sins. God forgave the city and spared it, and even let it exist for another five hundred years before the final judgement came and Nineveh was finally destroyed. What we are talking about here is that intercession has the capacity to change the way in which God will deal with a sinful nation, and instead of severe destruction, intercession could make the difference and open up the way for a spiritual revival to deal with the sins and the ungodliness of that nation.

That is why intercession is the most needed ministry in the world today, because only intercession has the capability of dealing with a whole nation and possibly turning a whole nation around and changing its course and destiny.

The second dynamic of intercession is that it has the ability to block the enemy from his activity against the Church. We remember that in Genesis 3:15, there was a prophecy given by the Lord concerning the work of the Church. It says that *"the seed of the woman should crush the head of the serpent,"* which is speaking about God giving the Church the authority to deal with the many schemes and attacks of the enemy upon her life and her work in the Kingdom. In the New Testament, the Lord Jesus is using this when speaking in Matthew 18:18–20 about binding and loosing. He says,

"Assuredly, I say to you, whatever you bind on earth will be bound in heaven, and whatever you loose on earth will be loosed in heaven. Again, I say to you that if two of you agree on earth concerning anything that they ask, it will be done for them by My Father in heaven. For where two or three are gathered together in My name, I am there in the midst of them."

When we talk about loosing and binding the powers of darkness, we need to remind ourselves that this is done only in the context of prayer. The Lord said that *"if two of you agree on earth concerning anything that they ask."* So, when we speak about spiritual warfare and about loosing and binding in the spiritual realm, let us not forget that this is not a kind of spiritual magic that we are trying to exercise, but a part of the ministry of intercession, and it has to do with agreeing together in prayer. In a later chapter, we will consider more closely the matter of united, corporate prayer by the Church. At this point, it is enough for us to consider the fact that the dynamics of intercession includes the possibility of withstanding and frustrating the powers of darkness as they try to come against the work of the Church.

This is confirmed further by another statement by the Lord Jesus in Matthew 16:18–19 where He responds to the confession of Simon Peter by saying,

"And I also say to you that you are Peter, and on this rock I will build My Church, and the gates of Hades shall not prevail against it. And I will give you the keys of the kingdom of heaven and whatever you bind on earth will be bound in heaven, and whatever you loose on earth will be loosed in heaven."

Notice that the Lord Jesus is speaking about the Church and about the gates of Hell. He is speaking about the conflict that there would be between the seed of the serpent and the seed of the woman as we read in Genesis 3:15. In other words, the Lord has given authority to His Church to be superior in the confrontation with the powers of evil. This is a work of the Church in the heavenly realms, in the unseen realm, and not a work that has to do with confronting people. That is the reason why we may assume that this has to do with the prayer ministry of the Church. If we think about it, there is hardly any any other way by which we might be able to move into the spiritual world than by prayer.

So, the dynamics of intercession include the capacity to deal with the powers of darkness as they seem to hinder the work of the Kingdom.

Another wonderful dynamic of the ministry of intercession is that it puts into operation the angelic forces. In James 5:16, the Apostle James speaks about the power of prayer in this very well-known scripture,

"The effective, fervent prayer of a righteous man avails much."

In one of the more recent English Bible translations, this has been translated as follows,

"The effective prayer of a righteous man stirs up much activity."

This understanding can also be found in the Amplified New Testament. What it really means is that when we move in intercessory prayer, we cause angelic forces to work on behalf of the Kingdom to accomplish the will of God. This is a very comforting thought. So often when we are joined with intercessors in the Church, we feel that we are but a small group, a minority, whereas in fact, we are far from a minority because the praying group of God's people is always linked up with the activity of the angels. As the matter of fact, when we are praying, God is commanding His angels to work on behalf of the saints.

This is quite clear when we look at the prayer life of Daniel. In the book of Daniel, we see that when Daniel gave himself to prayer and partial fasting, his prayer caused a battle to take place in the spiritual realm. From the first day that he turned his face towards God and began to seek the Lord in prayer, God sent His angel to deliver the answer. On the way down this angel was held up by a dark prince called the Prince of Persia and a battle took place where the messenger of God had to call back to heaven for help, and the archangel Michael had to come to his assistance. In the end the power of this dark Prince of Persia was overcome so that the angel could reach Daniel with God's message.

This is a perfect picture of what we are talking about here; our prayers will always cause angelic activity. So, we are not left alone but on the contrary are joining up with a vast host of angelic forces, who are ready to work at the command of our Lord. We on our part, are not able to command angels to go here or there. That thought is never found in the Bible. On the contrary, the Bible clearly states that the angels are the servants of the Lord of hosts and they obey His commandments. We are not to speak to the angels, and we are not to give the angels commandments. We are to speak to the Lord and to appeal to Him in prayer, and as a consequence of our intercession, the Lord in turn will command His angels to work on our behalf.

A final aspect of the dynamics of intercession is that intercession alone can produce an outpouring of the Holy Spirit. When we examine the New Testament in order to understand in which way the Holy Spirit is being poured out, we discover that this is the result of intercessory prayer. From both Acts 2, where the first outpouring of the Holy Spirit on the day of Pentecost is recorded, and Acts 4 where another outpouring of the Spirit upon the Church in Jerusalem is described, it is very clear that these outpourings of the Holy Spirit were the result of intercession made by the Church.

There is today a lot of misunderstanding as to how a revival can be brought about. Some Christians tend to believe that we might be able to bring about the release of the Holy Spirit by making some proclamations of faith or strong confessions, or even by directly commanding the Spirit to be released. In the New Testament, such an idea is totally unknown.

First of all, we are not able to take charge over the Holy Spirit and make Him obey our commands. It is actually the other way around; it is the Spirit who is supposed to be the Lord, and we are supposed to be subject to His will, and to His command. We are never in the Bible given any authority to handle the Holy Spirit, or to make Him move here and there or anywhere, or to cause the outpouring of His power by our choice. According to the Bible, the only way to see a true revival, which is the same as an outpouring of the Holy Spirit, is when the Church begins to engage in long-term united intercession.

We can see the same principle confirmed in every revival that has happened in the history of the Church. It does not matter what kind of revival we examine. We will see that the wind of the Spirit came as a result of intercessory prayer on behalf of the Church of Jesus Christ. We need to take that to heart and we also need to understand that today there is no other way in which we can possibly see a revival come about than the good, old biblical way. We need the Church to give herself to dedicated, persevering intercessory prayer before the Lord of the harvest, that He would pour out His Spirit and send out His workers to bring in the harvest.

Even if we consider a more personal approach to receiving the Holy Spirit, the New Testament teaching is very clear. The Apostle Peter says that the Lord gives the Holy Spirit to those who ask Him. We cannot by doing certain actions make sure that we receive the power of the Holy Spirit. It is when we turn to the Lord and we seek His face humbly that He will grant us the power of His Spirit.

Intercession as a Body Ministry

When reading through the New Testament, we discover that there is a vast difference between the promises for individual prayer and for corporate prayer. The promises God gives to His people when they pray together are much greater than those given for individual praying. Both in Acts 1:14 and 4:24, we read about *"praying with one accord,"* and in both cases the result is a major outpouring of the Holy Spirit. This could never be accomplished by people just praying on their own. It is when the Church begins to understand the power of joining together in unity and seeking the Lord with one mind and one soul that tremendous things can happen.

Generally speaking, this is a secret that has been lost in Western Christianity. It seems as if we have lost the understanding of corporateness, which really is the basic meaning of living in the New Covenant. In Africa and in the Far East, Christians have a much better understanding of the necessity and the power of moving together in the Church, but because of the great move of individualism in the Western world, the Church has basically lost its understanding of what it means to live together under the New Covenant.

That is the reason why much of Christianity in our part of the world is based more on Old Testament principles than on those of the New Testament. However, we should know why the Lord has established the New Covenant. Surely, He must have meant to go for some major changes, or He would probably just have kept the Old Covenant.

One of the basic differences between the Old and the New Covenant is that God is today desiring a people, not just a lot of individuals. God's way of working during Old Testament times was to use great individuals like the prophets, Isaiah, Jeremiah, Daniel and King David, Nehemiah and so on. But as we enter into the New Covenant, God's focus is no longer on great individuals, He is now seeking after a body.

It is my deep conviction that the New Testament must be read in the understanding of the body. The Scriptures of the New Testament are not just for individuals; they have been written for the whole, corporate body of God's people.

Under the Old Covenant, God had many faithful and great servants through whom He was able to reveal His divine will and accomplish His purposes upon the earth. But in the New Testament, God works according to the principle of the body. This was the great uniqueness about the day of Pentecost. The pentecostal experience was in its essence the birth of the body of Christ.

If we ask the question why God wants a body in the New Covenant, the answer is quite simple: only the body of Christ is able to fully express who Jesus is. No individual, however great and saintly, and holy and mature he or she might be, could ever express the personality of Jesus. He is far too great, far too rich and far too wonderful for any single person to express. It takes the whole body to reveal and manifest who the Person of the Lord Jesus is. That is why God wants to see His body united and built in the world because He has a desire to reveal His Son in the world.

It is for that purpose that the baptism of the Holy Spirit was given. The baptism of the Holy Spirit is not just for personal equipment to speak in tongues or exercise a charismatic gift, or even to have boldness to witness about Jesus. The real, deep significance of the pentecostal experience is found in Paul's first letter to the Corinthians 12:13 where it says, *"With one Spirit we were all baptized into one body."* God gave the outpouring of the Holy Spirit in order to make us able to be formed into a body that could function in unity and love. The birth of that wonderful body of Christ was on the day of Pentecost where this group of different people, by the outpouring of the Holy Spirit, were merged or melted together into a corporate body before God.

It was God's clear intention that we as believers under the New Covenant should live joined together as members of one another and learn to move together, to work together and do all the business of our Christian ministry together corporately. We have to admit that in the Western world, we have basically lost this concept. That is why it is so difficult for churches to attain to real unity and to learn to move together in the Spirit.

In many churches today the members, although belonging to the same local church, are very often divided into many different factions. There might be a group that is very much taken up with the worship, another one might feel the calling to pray, and yet another might be outgoing in evangelism, and so on.

Some years ago, I talked to a church pastor who had a church of about a thousand members. I had been invited to have a prayer seminar in his church, but when I entered the church on the eve of the seminar, I discovered that only a tiny part of the church – maybe about a hundred people – had come together to participate. However, during the prayer seminar, which took place in the main church hall, I could hear the sound of people singing in another part of the church building, and a little later a group of people came out and left the church.

This made me ask the pastor at the end of our meeting what was going on, and he kindly explained to me that in his church there were thirty-six different groups that were doing so-called "expert"-ministries. He added that he hardly ever saw the whole church come together in one gathering.

This is a typical picture of how we are running the Church in the Western world. I do not believe even for a moment that this was God's intention. He wanted us to learn to do everything together. In the early Church, when there was evangelism, the whole church was engaged in evangelism. When there was worship, the whole church was worshipping. When there was prayer, all the believers were together to seek the Lord. It is therefore true, I believe, to say that the New Testament concept is a corporate one, and that the language used in the New Testament must be understood as a body language. It is "we", not "I" who are in focus in the New Testament because the individual believer has now become a member of a body and so, his individuality does not matter so much anymore. It is the overall picture, it is the body that matters to God.

If we could learn to see this significant change from Old Covenant to New Covenant, it would be a great help for us as we seek to understand the real power of intercessory prayer.

It is interesting to notice that when Jesus in Matthew 18:18–20 speaks about the authority to bind and to loose, He is actually addressing the Church; He is speaking about what the Church can do, not what an individual can do. We need to understand that, otherwise we get wrong ideas about how spiritual authority can be properly exercised.

So, Jesus in Matthew 18 addresses the Church, and it is in these verses that He points out also that *"if two of you agree about anything on the earth, anything that they may ask shall be given to them by My Father who is in heaven."* Jesus does not say "if one of you is asking about anything, it shall be granted him or her," but He is stressing plurality here and is actually pointing out the least expression that you can have for the body; *"if two of you agree…".* And so, it is only in the corporate sense that binding and loosing is possible at all.

How much confusion there has been in the Church in recent years over this matter. How many individuals we see, who are jumping around in the world and trying by their own individual faith and power to bind great principalities and powerful angels of darkness. Actually, there is not in any place in the New Testament given that kind of authority to a single believer. It is all meant for the Church. The language is "we" and not "I". We are all individually church members, but it is the body that counts before God, and it is the body that He has chosen for His service in the world.

This is why the Lord Jesus also in verse 20 of this chapter says that it is where two or three are gathered in His name that He will manifest His presence. We need to understand that a single believer is very limited when it comes to manifesting the presence and the power of God. It is when we come together as the body – and the least expression of this is two or three – that we allow for the Lord to have the instrument through which He can manifest Himself in a fuller way.

Spiritual authority and prayer are linked together with the corporateness and the unity of the believers. Even when the Lord Jesus spoke about the nature of the Church long before the Church was born, He put forth this principle. In Matthew 16:18–20, Jesus is speaking about building His Church,

"I will build My Church, and the gates of Hades shall not prevail against it."

It is interesting to notice that the way the Lord is foreseeing the overthrow of the powers of darkness is through the building of His Church. He is not talking to Peter as an individual and giving him the authority to deal in his own being with the gates of Hell. This is a grave misunderstanding that individuals possess that power to take on the whole hierarchy of the devil. The chosen instrument for overcoming the powers of the enemy is the Church, and only as the Church is being built will there be the authority to frustrate and overcome the attempts of the enemy to come against God's purposes and God's plans. *"I will build My Church and the gates of Hell shall not prevail against it."*

So, when we speak about the power of prayer, we need to link it to learning to flow together in unity and harmony as believers, and to move together in one accord in our prayer ministry. There is no other way in which we can see the satanic power-structure being overcome and cast down from its position in the spiritual realm. The Church in the New Testament is central to everything that God has purposed to do in the world.

As we grow in our understanding and in our practice of

this corporateness in prayer, we will really come to see much more authority exercised towards the powers of the enemy, and also much more fruit brought forth in the life of the Church.

Prophetic Intercession

Living in the New Testament does not only mean that we need to see and to practise corporateness in what we are doing, it also means that we need to come under the direction and guidance of the Holy Spirit.

This principle applies, of course, to all aspects of Christian living, but it certainly also applies to the prayer-life of the believer. We are not supposed to be guided by any circumstances or even any needs when we intercede before God. We need to understand the guidance of the Holy Spirit, and submit to His will and His way.

In John's gospel 3:8, Jesus is outlining what it means to live in the New Covenant. He speaks about the Holy Spirit as the

"wind that blows wherever it wills, we do not know from where it comes or to where it goes, but we hear the sound. So it is with everybody who is born again of the Spirit."

A New Testament Christian is not supposed to be led or directed by rules or regulations from the outside, but he is supposed to learn to hear the voice of the Holy Spirit and to obey.

This means that we cannot base our intercession on our own understanding, our own good mind, or just any available information, but we need to learn how to wait upon the Holy Spirit and to make ourselves available and ready to move together with Him.

So often, we are controlled by our own mind, or even by our traditions and the theology in which we were brought up. But Jesus tells us that we cannot possibly by our natural mind know the ways of the Spirit. We cannot know from where He comes, and we cannot know to where He goes. It is for us to become sensitive and to hear His voice and just learn to obey Him. It makes us pretty much flexible before God, both in our lives, and also when we come to seek Him in prayer.

We need to be able to put aside all preconceived ideas and even all the important prayer-subjects that we have come up with on our own, to listen to what the Holy Spirit is saying and learn what the possible burden is that He has for prayer. Only in this way can we hope to be really effective in what we are doing as intercessors.

To learn how to really exercise the ministry of intercession will require our complete dependency on the Holy Spirit. His role is crucial if we aim at getting through and touching God in our prayers.

In Hebrews 8:11, the writer gives a very remarkable statement about the New Covenant. He says that

"none of them shall teach his neighbour, and none his brother, saying, 'Know the Lord' for all shall know Me, from the least of them to the greatest of them."

Does this mean that there will be no need in the New Testament Church for instruction or teaching? Certainly not. But it does mean that anybody who is instructing anyone in the Church must be aware of the fact that his mission is not to take the place of the Holy Spirit in the believer's life, but through his teaching, actually push the believer closer and closer into dependency on hearing the voice of the Holy Spirit and understanding the way that the Spirit is leading his life from within.

This is actually the essence of the New Covenant; that everybody can know the Lord Himself, everybody can hear the Lord, and our job, if we are teachers of the Word of God, is not to try and convince other people about our particular theology, but by our teaching and instruction enable the believers themselves to find their own way to communicate with the Lord and to hear the voice of His Spirit.

One of the absolute basics about true intercession is not so much, therefore, whether we can learn to listen and hear the voice of God. That is actually very simply what we understand by "prophetic prayer". Prophecy means to come to know what is in the heart of God for the moment. It is not so much knowing things in the future or to be able to explain eschatological truth in the end times. To be prophetic is to be someone who can interpret what is moving in the heart of God for the very moment, and so, prophetic prayer means that we are able to discern the burdens which are upon God's heart in order that we might join with Him in our prayers.

Paul speaks about the role of the Holy Spirit in the prayer-life of the Church from Romans 8:26–27.

"Likewise the Spirit also helps in our weaknesses, for we do not know what we should pray for as we ought, but the Spirit Himself makes intercession for us with groanings which cannot be uttered. Now He who searches the heart knows what the mind of the Spirit is because He makes intercession for the saints according to the will of God."

We learn from these scriptures that the role of the Spirit in the life of intercession cannot be underestimated. Actually, if it is not by the Spirit that we are praying and interceding, we are just performing the works of the flesh, which availeth nothing.

Paul says that *"we do not know what we should pray for as we ought;"* this is actually a very important basis to have for our prayer-life. We need to be aware of the fact that there is no way we can figure out the right way of praying for certain things or persons by our natural mind. Only as we come in touch with the Holy Spirit will we be able to really understand the issues properly. *"We do not know what we should pray for as we ought,"* but *"the Spirit helps our weaknesses."*

For those of us who feel that we are certainly weak when it comes to the life of prayer and intercession, there is good news. Prayer and intercession are for people who know their own weakness and who know how dependent they are on the help of the Holy Spirit. Those who are able to do things by their own intelligence and their own strength are simply not qualified for the life of prayer. For we cannot know what we should pray for out of our own understandings. We need revelation and direction from the Holy Spirit. He, the Holy Spirit, is the one who knows the will of God in every circumstance, in every situation, in every case for which we might be interceding. He searches the hearts and He is able to discern the truth in each and every case.

Paul actually points out in these verses that real intercession is not that "I am praying my stuff towards God" – however important that might be or however important I might think my prayer subjects might be. That is not real intercession. Intercession is when we see ourselves as instruments that will allow the Spirit to actually pray within us according to the will of God, and this is a situation where the burden of the Holy Spirit can be felt so strongly that we are not even able to utter any words.

Many believers believe that prayer is the ability to express a lot of words before God. But this is far from being the truth. Prayer is the expression of the Holy Spirit, the manifestation of the Holy Spirit within our innermost being, and sometimes that manifestation is not even able to be expressed by words. It is just something that is so heavy that it can only be expressed by groanings which cannot be uttered.

As we come together to pray as a body of believers, we need to exercise much sensitivity to come to sense the burdens of the Holy Spirit. Otherwise we might just waste our time doing our own thing.

"The wind is blowing," the Lord Jesus said, *"you do not know from where it comes, and you do not know to where it goes, but you hear the sound. So it is with everyone who is born again by the Spirit."*

We need to be open for things that we have not thought about; things that have not come up in our own minds. We need to make ourselves available before the Lord so that we can begin to sense the burdens that are upon His heart.

Let me give you a practical example of prophetic prayer. Many years ago, when we had our prayer-ministry going on in my local church in Copenhagen, the Lord was teaching us this matter of being sensitive to the voice of the Holy Spirit. Normally as the pastor, I would always prepare our prayer meeting very well. I would even speak out some very important prayer issues that I felt we needed to work on in prayer. I remember one evening going to the prayer meeting with my usual prayer subjects ready to share with the church, but then something unusual happened.

At that time, we had learned that before we would start to go to work in prayer, we needed to give time to wait upon the Lord in silent worship and adoration. As we were spending that time before the Lord, all of a sudden the Holy Spirit moved upon one of our sisters, who began to weep and cry and come under the power of the Spirit. She then began to prophesy and issue a strong call to our church to pray for our brothers and sisters in China.

Normally, I would be very sceptical about taking guidance after just a prophecy, but that evening I was convinced that it was the Holy Spirit. I have never seen a woman come under the burden of the Spirit in that way. It was just as if she was in birth pangs, trembling in pain. Nobody at that time had ever dreamed or thought about praying for the church in China. We had come together to pray for Denmark as we usually did once a week. But the call of the Spirit was so strong that we had to put aside all our well-intentioned prayer issues and just give ourselves to crying out to the Lord for our suffering brothers and sisters in China.

We actually went on non-stop in a flow for more than three hours, interceding for people we did not even know. Just by the burden of the Holy Spirit we were able to pray with tremendous power and conviction. This is what we understand by prophetic prayer.

Of course, there is also another way of understanding this point. To be able to flow with the Holy Spirit today means that we must have an understanding of what God is doing in the world in our day. And God is actually doing specific things. We could also say that God is today doing things that are different from those He did in the previous generation, or those He worked on in the beginning of this century.

It is therefore of the utmost importance that we as believers come to understand what God is doing in the world today, among the nations, in our own nation, and in the Church, in order that we might be prophetic in our praying.

The whole point of intercession is to work together with God for the fulfilment of His purposes in the world. And how would we be able to do that if we don't even have the simplest clue about what God is doing in our present-day situation?

Let me suggest to you a few major things that I believe that the

Holy Spirit is doing right now in the world.

First of all, I am convinced that we are living in those days as foretold by the scriptures when the Great Commission shall be fulfilled and the Gospel shall be preached to all the tribes, tongues and nations on the earth. Actually, in Matthew 24:14, Jesus Himself in His great speech about the end-times says that

"this Gospel of the Kingdom must be preached as a testimony unto all the nations, and then the end shall come."

If we really believe that we are living in the end-time, then we also must believe that this is the work of the Holy Spirit today to bring the gospel of the Lord Jesus Christ to all the unreached people groups, tongues and tribes who have not yet heard about the salvation of God.

Now, if this is true, then this area becomes very prophetic and becomes a priority for us in our intercession, and if we give ourselves to work on that which is prophetic; that which is God's burden and His priority on the earth, then, of course, we will experience an entering into the flow of the Holy Spirit and a coming under the anointing of the power of the Holy Spirit. And this is actually the secret of successful intercession; that we are working, not on things that we feel are important, but on things that God considers important, and that which He is working on today among the nations.

World evangelism today is a major area for intercessors to take on. But we have to understand it rightly. It is not a matter of the preaching of the gospel to the same people over and over again. It is a matter of the gospel being preached to all the unreached peoples first.

If the Church is only evangelizing the same areas over and over again, we are not really being prophetic. The Lord did not say that in this age of the Church and of the Holy Spirit He was going to save all the nations and the people within them. He said that He wanted a testimony to be raised in each and every nation, and from that we can assume that He wants His Church to be planted in each and every nation on the earth. And since we have several thousand unreached people groups in the world today who have not even heard the name of Jesus, we still have a lot of work that we need to conclude. And this must have priority; to pray for the gospel to break through to the unreached peoples before we get involved for the hundredth time in preaching to the same people again.

Among intercessors in the world today, this point has been strongly highlighted by the Holy Spirit. And today we have prayer movements who are specifically working on raising up prayer in the Church of Jesus Christ for all these unreached people groups. Also, we have many individual churches who are adopting an unreached tribe to pray and intercede for, and also to send missionaries with the gospel to. This is clearly a prophetic area, and this is where we can practise prophetic prayer.

Another area is the unity of the Body of Christ. In my mind, there is no doubt that this is a high priority in the heart of God for these last days. It is not only the desire of God to answer the prayers of His dearly beloved Son, the Lord Jesus, *"that they all may be one,"* but it is also a matter that needs to be resolved before the coming again of the Lord Jesus. I do not believe that Jesus is coming back to fetch a divided, depressed, miserable and spiritually poor Church. I believe that Jesus is coming to get a glorious Church. A Church that is called His Bride, who has made herself ready for the great day of the heavenly wedding to her heavenly bridegroom.

If that is so, we certainly need to generate a lot of prayer for the unity of the Church to become a reality. Let us look at some scriptures in the following pages, to confirm this matter in our hearts. Praying for the unity in the Body of Christ is a high priority at this time in God's heart and therefore it is prophetic praying.

In these last days of this age, the Holy Spirit is working strongly, I believe, to perfect the Church. And if the Church is going to be made ready for the soon coming of her Head and Lord, it certainly means that true unity has to be established between the different parts of the Body of Christ.

There are different views as to what kind of Church will be living at the time of the return of the Lord Jesus. Some Christians tend to believe that because it will be a very difficult time with many trials and testing and going through the fire, the Church in the last days cannot be expected to be an overcoming one, but rather must concentrate on surviving against the increasing pressure of satanic opposition. Although it is very true that the last days will be extremely difficult and much more so than in any other period of the life of the Church, this is still not the biblical perspective; that Jesus is coming to rescue a miserable group of Christians who are struggling just to survive.

The New Testament picture of the Church is by and large that Jesus has offered up His life to get Himself a glorious Church, as it is put in Ephesians 5:27. Jesus is not coming back to get a divided, depressed and beaten Church. Jesus is coming back to get a glorious Church, a Bride who has adorned herself and made herself ready for her Husband.

> *"Let us be glad and rejoice and give Him glory, for the marriage of the Lamb has come, and His wife has made herself ready."* (Revelation 19:7)

We are entitled to expect that when a bride is making herself ready for her wedding, she certainly would never look miserable, worn out, depressed or scattered, but she would stand in the glory of her beauty and youth. And this is the picture of the Church; a glorious Church which is existing in the last days just before the return of the Lord Jesus.

However, if the Church is going to be a glorious Church, it must be one of unity. When Jesus in John's gospel 17:22 speaks about his intercession for the unity of the Church, His Body, He says as follows:

"And the glory which you gave Me I have given them that they may be one just as We are One."

It is interesting to notice that Jesus connects glory with unity. He says that the glory He received from His Father He gave to His disciples, to His Church in order to make them one. That means that whenever the Church is flowing in unity, it reflects the glory of the Lord Jesus. On the other hand, if there is no unity in the Body of Christ, then there is no glory either, no matter how much we try to proclaim it to be so. Unity and glory go together, and the Lord Jesus gave His glory to the Church in order that they may be one.

In that light, the unity of the Body becomes a high priority in the heart of God because a glorious Church in these last days means a Church flowing in unity, and a Body of Christ that is flowing in love for one another. And, if Jesus is to have a glorious Church, the unity of the Church becomes maybe the highest priority for intercessory prayer at this time, as we believe He is returning soon.

The Lord Jesus Himself devoted His last high-priestly prayer on earth to that cause, and we can be sure that this is a major burden upon God's heart for today. This in turn means that the Holy Spirit is working towards this goal among the believers all over the world. If we want to be prophetic, we need to give ourselves in prayer for that objective to be fulfilled, and as we go along that path, we will enjoy and experience the anointing of the Holy Spirit.

It has been my joy to register on my many travels around the world, that whenever God's people are flowing with the work of the Holy Spirit, they come under the anointing of the Spirit in a special way.

I have seen churches who might have taken it upon themselves to pray for unreached people groups, and the result has been a tremendous blessing by God, who in turn has given growth to their church without any special evangelistic effort on their part.

In the same way, I have witnessed how churches would give themselves in a special way to praying for the unity of the believers in their local area, and likewise experience great blessings and spiritual growth, also without any special evangelistic effort.

In my own church back in Copenhagen, we had an experience in that area. As we went on praying in the church every week, the Lord began to teach us that He did not want us to make our own church and our own church affairs the first and foremost priority for our prayer ministry, but, on the contrary, He put on my heart as the pastor to instruct the people to always remember the principle "to pray for somebody else's church before you pray for your own."

In this way, the Lord laid on our hearts regularly to pray for the other churches in our area of Copenhagen, and that one factor caused a lot of blessing to come upon us. In the course of four years, our little church grew from eighty members to about three hundred, again, without any special evangelistic effort.

I am not saying that we do not need evangelistic effort and that we do not need to preach the gospel. We do. But I am saying that an even more effective way to grow is by coming under the anointing of the Holy Spirit. This happens when we discover the prophetic issues that the Holy Spirit is working on today.

A third point concerning prophetic prayer to be considered here is the question of the restoration of Israel. When we are talking about what God is doing in the world today at this time, it is quite evident that the Holy Spirit is working to restore the nation of Israel, to bring back the Jewish people to their ancient land, and to prepare Israel for the coming of their Messiah and for the role that Israel is going to play in the coming age of the Kingdom of God.

Unfortunately, there are quite a few people, both evangelical and charismatic, in the Church who have no understanding or vision for God's dealings with the Jewish people. In a word in Acts 3:21, the Bible says that

"heaven must receive the Lord Jesus until the times of restoration of all things which God has spoken by the mouth of all His holy prophets since the world began."

In other words, the coming of the Lord Jesus is linked to the fulfilment of the prophetic scriptures. Notice that it speaks about what God has spoken about by the mouth of all His holy prophets since the world began. This means that we must include the Old Testament scriptures, and we need to remember that the time when this scripture was written, all the Church really had was the Old Testament. It is amazing to see today how the prophecies of the Old Testament are being fulfilled, one after another.

Intercessors are called to work in prayer for the fulfilment of every prophecy that has been spoken by God through the mouth of these holy prophets.

This was how it was with Daniel. When he discovered while reading Jeremiah that the time for the end of the Babylonian captivity had come, he gave himself to intercession and fasting for twenty-one days in order to pave the way for this prophecy to be fulfilled.

Real intercession is nothing but working together with God for the realization of everything that He has foretold in His Word. It is amazing that so much of what has happened was foretold hundreds of years ago before it really occurred.

Isn't it fantastic that the prophet Micah in his fifth chapter is able to prophesy that the Messiah of Israel would be born in the tiny little town of Bethlehem? And so five hundred years later, Jesus was born in Bethlehem. We would not have wondered so much if the Word had told us that Jesus would be born in one of the major cities of the ancient world. But when it comes to such a little village as Bethlehem, then it is an amazing testimony of the accuracy and truthfulness of the Word of God.

Also, the prophet Isaiah in his fifty-third chapter speaks with great accuracy about the sufferings of the coming Messiah on the cross. There is hardly anyone in the evangelical church who would not agree that this is true. But strangely enough, when it comes to the prophecies about the people of Israel, and the return of the Jews to their homeland, all of a sudden there is great confusion, and many leading people in the church are spiritualizing these prophecies to the extent that they claim that these prophecies deal with the Church.

How is it though, that the prophecies about Jesus being born in Bethlehem and his sufferings later on the cross of Calvary need to be understood literally, whereas the prophecies of old concerning the Jewish people and their return to their homeland, and the restoration of Israel happening before the return of the Messiah, are spiritualized instead, and applied to the Church?

Well, the Church has never been dispersed to the ends of the earth and there is no homeland that all Christians ought to return to. It simply does not make sense that some prophecies can be agreed upon to be true and others are being spiritualized. The Lord has said that Jesus will be held back in heaven until the times of restoration of all things which God has spoken by the mouth of all His Holy prophets since the world began. Therefore, Israel is being restored, and the Jewish people are returning by the thousands in these years, and God is going to fulfil every word He spoke about His ancient people, the Jewish people.

That being so, it means that this is something that the Holy Spirit is working powerfully to perform in the world today. And if we want to be in the flow of the Holy Spirit, then we need to give ourselves in prayer and intercession to work on this issue.

Also in this area, we have seen how the Church receives blessing when it takes up the burdens of the Holy Spirit in the world. There are examples of churches that have started to pray for Israel regularly, who, like Daniel, are calling upon the Lord to fulfil His promises to the Jewish people; and how they have entered into a new anointing under the power of the Spirit. It is as if that anointing that comes from praying prophetically is spilling over, as it were, to other areas of the work of the church.

Once we have noticed where the wind is blowing, and we have become obedient to follow His flow, there is a force operating in our lives that will enable us to be successful in almost anything that we are doing in our work for the Kingdom.

Being Available

We are talking about the keys to powerful intercession. The difficulties for Christians to enter into intercession are not so much in the area of "knowhow" as to how to actually perform this ministry, but they stem from a lack of preparation and a failure to enter into the presence of the Lord.

The problem is not so much that we are not praying, but that we are praying the wrong way, that we are stuck in our own thoughts, and that we have difficulties getting in touch with the Holy Spirit as we enter into intercession.

Very often what takes the longest time in the process of prayer is for us to be unloaded from all our own burdens and our own thoughts, including all our anxieties and needs, and come to the place where we are really empty and available for the Holy Spirit to put upon us prayers that are according to the will of God.

If we really want to enter into the Holy Spirit and touch the presence of the Lord in our intercession, there is a certain matter that we need to pay attention to.

In Romans 12:1–3, the Apostle Paul is pointing out the basis of all true ministry. *"I beseech you therefore, brethren, by the mercies of God, that you present your bodies a living sacrifice, holy, acceptable to God, which is your reasonable service. And do not be conformed to this world, but be transformed by the renewing of your mind, that you may prove what is that good and acceptable and perfect will of God. For I say, through the grace given to me, to everyone who is among you, not to think of himself more highly than he ought to think, but to think soberly, as God has dealt to each one a measure of faith."*

It has been a great privilege in my life to know a very great servant of the Lord, who is now with the Lord. This man was Peter van Woerden, who was the nephew of Corrie ten Boom, whose family took care of so many Jewish people and hid them from the Nazis during the Second World War.

I came to know Peter some years ago, and we became very close friends, perhaps in a special way, because we both suffered from heart problems. Peter was a very unique man. He was able so often in a simple manner to put his finger upon the essential things.

The Lord healed me from my sickness in 1989 and I met Peter later the same year. Before my healing I had been caught up in seven different ministries or responsibilities, but after my sickness and subsequent healing, I had only one left; that of being the international co-ordinator of Intercessors International. At the time, when I met Peter, I had just had a new business card printed, and so during our brief talk, I handed him one in order that he might have our new address and telephone number in Germany.

However, Peter looked at the card and then smiled and looked back at me and said, "Johannes, it says here that you are the international co-ordinator of the prayer movement. You can't really be that, only the Holy Spirit can co-ordinate the prayer movement in the world!"

I couldn't help but smile at his very true comment and said, "Well, Peter, I guess you are right. But you know, this is about the last piece of ministry that I have, so if you take this away from me, I have absolutely nothing."

We both laughed and I curiously asked him then what kind of

ministry he had. At first he looked a little surprised, then he said, "If I told you the kind of ministry I have, I am not sure you would believe me." I replied that I would like to know about it anyway, and then came his unique answer, "I have the ministry of availability!"

I said to Peter, "I haven't heard about that ministry before. You better tell me what that is," and so he gave me an example of what it means to be available for God.

Years ago, when he and his wife went to Jerusalem to get a flat to live in part-time for their ministry, the Lord led them to a small house in the Christian quarter of the Old City in Jerusalem. As they moved in, they asked the Lord to show them where He would have them worship Him and what kind of church they should be attending. Meanwhile, Peter in his imagination had already hoped that they would be a part of the more lively, evangelical churches in Jerusalem, but the Lord had something different in mind and answered very clearly that they should attend the services in the small, Syrian orthodox church that was right below their flat. They were very surprised.

First of all, they had not even noticed such a church below them, and secondly, they had no idea of how to worship in a Syrian orthodox church. However, they decided to obey the Lord and started going to that little church. They did not understand what the priest was saying or doing, as he was standing and performing his ministry in front of the altar, and besides, they were the only people that ever attended the church. So, they decided that they would intercede and pray for the priest during the ministry times.

A couple of months went by, during which they came regularly to worship the Lord and pray in that little church. But then, one Sunday, Peter was unable to go, as he fell sick, and his wife decided to stay home and take care of him. And as they returned the following Sunday, the priest came down for the first time after the service to talk to them. He looked very bleak as he asked them, "Where were you last Sunday? You are not going to leave me, are you?" Then Peter said to his wife, "Let us put our hands upon this man and pray for him," and as they did this, the Holy Spirit came upon this Syrian orthodox priest and he was met by

God, born again, and also at the same time filled with the Holy Spirit and became a completely different person.

This is what happens when we become completely available to the Holy Spirit. This is also what Paul speaks about as being the very foundation of any ministry in the body of Christ. We are to present our bodies a living sacrifice and put it on the altar before God. Because when you are laid on the altar as a living sacrifice, you become available for God. In the Old Testament days when they sacrificed animals on the altar, they had to bind the animal to the horns of the altar because it would instinctively sense what was about to happen, and of course, would not be content to just lie there passively, waiting to be killed, but would have jumped off the altar at the first given opportunity. Therefore, the animal was tied to the horns of the altar.

Once we lie on the altar of God, we can no longer do our own thing, we can no longer go our own ways. We have to lie there silently, waiting for God to move.

Paul says that we should not be conformed to this world, but be transformed by the renewing of our minds so that we might be able to understand what is the will of God. And this is exactly the point that we are talking about here. As we come before God in intercession, our greatest need is to be delivered from everything that will defile us from the world; worldly thoughts, worldly motives, and that we be renewed in our minds so that we can discern the will of the Lord in each and every case. Only when we have come to that point where we have put all things down before God and are waiting upon Him, have we reached the place where true intercession can begin.

When Paul and his co-workers were praying in Acts 13, it says that they were ministering unto the Lord and fasting, which means that they were just seeking the face of the Lord; they were just entering into His presence. They did not have any specific subject for their prayers. It was during a time like this, as recorded in Acts 13:1–3, that they entered into the presence of the Lord and the Holy Spirit began to move and call Paul and Barnabas to become the first missionaries to Europe.

I am absolutely convinced that when Paul and the other apostles and servants of the Lord met that day in Antioch, they were not there to discuss how they could best bring the gospel to Europe. I don't even think it was in their minds. What they were taken up with was a desire to seek the Lord, to worship Him, and to come before Him and be available for whatever purpose He might have for them in their ministry. It was out of that availability that the gospel for the first time came to the European continent.

Some years ago, I met a pastor from Norway who sought my advice on a problem he had in his prayer-life. Every time he would come before the Lord, he felt bombarded by so many things that needed to be covered in prayer. While he was praying, he would think about what he was supposed to speak on the next morning in church; what needed to be written in the next church bulletin; where they would be able to get the money from to pay their bills; and he would think of all the various needs in his family and his ministry. And so, before he knew of it, he was so frustrated that he would actually give up trying to come through in prayer.

When I listened to him, it struck me that this pastor did not really know the nature of true prayer, and I said to him that he needed to understand that prayer is not our bringing before the Lord all the things that we think are important; but prayer is our coming to the point where we are available to listen to what the Lord wants us to deal with in prayer, whatever that might be. If we cannot learn to empty ourselves before God and unwind our busy minds and put down every anxious thought that we might have, we will never come to the place where we will be able to allow the Holy Spirit to begin to inspire us and help us in prayer.

We need to have our minds renewed. We need to know what it is to empty ourselves before God and just come to the point where we can say with the prophet, "Lord, here I am." We are only instruments and vessels for the Holy Spirit. We are not the ones who are supposed to initiate the process of prayer; that part belongs to the Holy Spirit.

In John 15:16, the Lord Jesus says these words,

"You did not choose Me, but I chose you and appointed you that you should go and bear fruit and that your fruit should

remain, that whatever you ask the Father in my name, He may give you."

It seems unnecessary in a way that the Lord should even say that we did not choose Him, but that He chose us. But as a matter of fact, it is important for that to be underlined because many of us often act as if we had really chosen God for our purposes and our needs, instead of realizing that He is the one who has chosen us for His purposes and for His needs.

Jesus says here that He appointed us that we should go and bear fruit and that our fruit should remain so that whatever we ask the Father in His name He might give to us. It is only as we are in that to which we are being appointed, that we are able to bear fruit. This is an important principle and also applies to intercession.

The total success of intercessory prayer depends on the source of our intercession, whether the things we are interceding for have been appointed by God, or whether they are of our own choice, our own emotions, or our own burdens. If they come from ourselves and we try to get the Lord to go along with them, it is in fact us who are choosing Him for that which we feel is important. But when we are in that to which He appoints us, we will see fruit of our labour; we will receive answers to our prayers, and the outcome of our intercessory ministry will be fruit for eternity; fruit that will remain.

This is the secret of this amazing statement that *"whatever you ask the Father in My name, He will give it to you."* If we do not understand this promise in this context, we can easily be deceived into thinking that whatever we might think that we would like to ask the Lord, He has already promised that He would give to us. That is not what it says. It says that when we are in that to which He appointed us, then we will bear fruit, and then we can ask the Lord whatever we want, and it shall be given unto us.

In the light of intercession, we cannot just plunge into each and every thing that we feel is necessary, or that other people think that we really need to intercede for. We have to understand that we have been chosen by the Lord Jesus and that He has appointed us to certain things and we need to remain within His appointment. Then we shall see fruit and whatever we ask His

Father shall be given unto us.

This is why we need to come before the Lord and make ourselves available for that which is of Him; that which is according to His will. We need to be transformed from the defilement of this world and be renewed in our minds so that we can discern the good, and the acceptable, and the perfect will of God.

A very well-known intercessor said to me many years ago, "The most important thing about prayer is to make sure that you are coming into the presence of the Lord, and from there the Holy Spirit will lead you and guide you and give you His burden." He also said that if you have ten minutes available to pray, then use the first eight minutes to be still and empty yourself before God and worship Him. Then the remaining two minutes in intercessory prayer will be tremendously effective.

We need to understand that nothing with our God is by coincidence. Everything with God goes according to His pre-prepared plan. In Ephesians 2:8 Paul says that *"we have been saved by grace through faith"* and that it is a gift of God and we cannot deserve it. And then in verse 10, he goes on saying that

"we are his workmanship, created in Christ Jesus for good works which God prepared beforehand that we should walk in them."

The amazing thing about our salvation is that not only are we saved by grace, but God has also, as it were, saved our very lives. He has prepared our lives in Christ Jesus for good works which were already ordained before the foundation of the world. This is the true meaning of this scripture according to the original; that God even before the foundation of the world not only chose us to become His children, but He also planned and prepared our very lives, even to the detail of the good works that we were supposed to do.

Just think about it; every day God has prepared our lives, the people that we are going to meet, the actions that we are going to take, the decisions that we need to make. All of that is not just happening by coincidence. It is a well-prepared plan that God a long time ago put together for our lives, as truly as we are in Christ, and we are following Him.

41

The real thing for us then is to discover God's plan, and that is why we need to come to this decision of availability. We need to come before the Lord and just discover what He has planned for us for each and every day. And this is precisely the same when we speak about intercession; that we come to the point where we can discern and discover God's plan for our prayer meeting or our prayer time together, that we can come to believe and trust in the fact that God has already beforehand prepared what we are going to do, what we are going to say, what we are going to pray.

In my earlier days in the ministry, including the prayer ministry, I always used to prepare well for everything that I was going to be a part of. I think I inherited from my father's German background a good, logical, and systematic German mind, and I remember how I made a lot of effort to have everything under control and to know what I was supposed to do at the various occasions. I don't believe it is wrong to prepare oneself, I don't even believe it is wrong to be systematic in one's work, but I do believe that all of that can become an enemy of really understanding the way of the Spirit and grasping the burden that God has upon His heart for the moment.

Before I entered my years of sickness, I was one of the most systematic, well-planned Bible teachers you could ever dream of. I was at that time engaged in seven spiritual leadership-responsibilities and ministries, but when I was put through the fire and three years of non-stop pain and depression, I lost all of these seven. However, I remember that when the Lord healed me on that Saturday morning in February in 1989, my heart was full of expectation that the Lord would restore to me all of the ministry opportunities that I had lost and even add some more to the list.

As I was seeking the Lord for what He would have me do in the future, He clearly said to me that He was not going to give me back my seven lost ministry opportunities. He gave me a word from Ephesians 2:10, pointing out that I need not be worried about what to do for Him or engage myself in endless activity to serve Him in as many areas as possible and the best I could. This was not necessary. He had His own plan that was thought out and well-planned even before the foundation of the world, and He clearly said to me that the way He wanted me to live in my new resurrection was just day by day to discover that which He had prepared, and do the things that He would quicken my heart to do, and go to the places that He would give me a burden for, and not in any way try to organize my own ministry anymore.

I was to become completely available for Him and be able to be in the position where I would go wherever He wanted to send me, and do exactly what was upon His heart. That position before God is the very foundation for an effective intercessory ministry.

Do Not Cast Away Your Confidence

Intercession cannot be learned by just using certain manuals or methods. Intercession is a ministry that flows out of our very relationship with God. When we speak and teach about intercession, we are bound, therefore, to take up certain areas of our relationship with the Lord as this will influence our ability to enter into real intercession.

One such area deals with our ability to trust in the Lord. Generally speaking, prayer in the New Testament is rather pointless unless we believe. Time after time, the New Testament writers underline that when we pray we must believe that we are being heard by our Father in heaven, and being heard by Him means that we will also receive that which we ask of Him.

The Apostle James speaks about praying the "prayer of faith", and in the beginning of the epistle of James says that when we ask we must believe, because a man who has doubt is like a wave of the sea, and no-one with that kind of an attitude can expect to receive anything from the Lord.

Faith is absolutely crucial to our whole prayer-life. In Hebrews 10:35, the writer is giving us this exhortation, *"Do not cast away your confidence, because it has a great reward."* This is, of course, a principle that could be applied to all aspects of Christian living and certainly, it does apply very much to prayer.

It is not so much what we utter in prayer to the Lord that matters, as it is the condition of our heart that counts before the

Lord. The question is whether we pray with a heart of confidence, or whether we just pray out of a necessity or a need, or even out of a religious habit. Unless there is trust in our hearts in the Lord, prayer does not really pay off. That is why Hebrews 10:35 speaks about a reward.

In fact, many of us who have unanswered prayers in our lives ought to examine our hearts as to whether there is unbelief and distrust in them when we come before the Lord to pray. Because unless we honour the Lord by trusting fully in Him, God is not able to give us any reward and any answer to our prayers.

Whenever we have thrown away our confidence, all we do in our Christian lives, including all our prayers, is rather pointless and useless, and there is no promise that God will give heed to our requests. In such a situation, prayer and intercession become nothing but religious habits, and for that kind of exercise no spiritual fruit can be expected.

Also in Hebrews 11:6, the writer is pointing out the great importance of having faith; having trust in the Lord,

"But without faith it is impossible to please Him for he who comes to God must believe that He is and that He is a rewarder of those who diligently seek Him."

In other words, if there is no trusting heart behind our prayer, there will be no reward either. This word does not speak about believing in the existence of God because a lot of people do believe that God exists, even those who have no relationship with Him, and the scriptures even say that *"the demons believe that God exists and they tremble."* It is not a matter of having faith in the existence of God, but it is a matter of having faith in the character of God. *"He who comes to God must believe that He is"* meaning that He is the one that He says He is. We all know that one of the Lord's names is *"the great I AM"* and it speaks about His character.

As we come before the Lord to require of Him, the key to our success will be whether we have a heart that is trusting in the character of God. So, in other words, it is not so much what we do before God that will bring us the things that we need, as it is the heart-attitude that we have before the Lord. It is a question of having faith or no faith when we appear before the throne of God in prayer.

In the Lord's prayer, which we find in Matthew 6, it says in the sixth verse,

"But you when you pray go into your room and when you have shut your door, pray to your Father who is in the secret place, and your Father who sees in secret will reward you openly."

Again, we see that the Lord Jesus is speaking about "prayer" and "reward". It is the very meaning of prayer that we should get a reward when we come with our requests to the Lord.

We might wonder why it is that the Lord is advising us to go into our room and shut our door, and to be alone with our Father who is in the secret place. But I am sure that again this has to do with God wanting to have our hearts exposed before Him, because as long as we are together with other people and other believers, for instance if we are taking part in a corporate prayer gathering, the fellowship will easily stimulate us to pretend in a lot of ways and we cannot be honest or naked in our hearts before God. So, the Father wants us to have that experience of coming before Him, being alone. And when we are alone with the Lord, it is quite obvious that we are in a much more honest position without any outward stimulation at all. The Lord wants to see our hearts; He wants to know whether we are trusting in Him, whether we have full confidence in His character, and then He will reward us according to our prayers.

It is amazing how much unbelief there is in our hearts as believers, even in the realm of prayer. In Mark 11, Jesus is walking with His disciples towards Jerusalem, and as they pass by Bethany, Jesus feels hungry but sees a small fig-tree and goes to this tree in order to find some fruit. But as He does not find any fruit, He issues a curse and says to the fig-tree, *"Never again shall anybody eat fruit from you."* All the disciples were together with the Lord Jesus at this time and of course they may have wondered what on earth was going on.

First of all, why would Jesus curse the fig-tree because it didn't have the fruit He was seeking? Because in the natural, the Word says it was not even the season for fruit.

Secondly, they must have wondered as Jesus spoke His curse

against the tree, why nothing seemed to happen immediately. It is only as they come back the same way the following day and they pass by that same fig-tree, that Peter notices with great surprise that the fig-tree has withered. He points it out to the Lord Jesus and by this actually exposes the unbelief in his heart. Had he trusted in the character of the Lord Jesus when He spoke forth the curse the previous day, he would have known that whatever the Lord Jesus says will be fulfilled. There would then not have been any big fuss when they discovered that the fig-tree had withered away. However, because there was no trust in his heart, he was taken completely by surprise.

When believers are surprised to see miracles taking place, it exposes the spirit of unbelief dwelling in their hearts.

If word got around that great miracles were taking place in a particular church in the city, you can be sure that a lot of believers would make a pilgrimage to that church the following Sunday just to investigate the sensational events. However, if we had hearts of faith, we would not be so greatly surprised and miracles, wonders and healings would be something normal in the life of the Church, just as it was in the days of the early Church.

The Lord Jesus' response to the outburst of Peter is this, *"Have faith in God."* In other words, Jesus is pointing His finger at the central point, namely having faith in God. Peter did not have this faith, and this is why he was overcome by surprise. In the original Greek, there is an alternative way of translating this phrase, "Have faith in God," and it goes like this, "Have God's faith." And this brings forth even more the exact meaning of what Jesus said.

What we need is not so much human faith, but we need that divine faith which is given by the Holy Spirit, which is God's very own faith.

In a time when there is so much talk in the Body of Christ about faith, it is important to mention this distinction. Because if we are only talking about human faith, we are going to be disappointed in the long run, because human faith will not hold and is bound to fail. Every human being has a portion of so-called "natural faith." If this wasn't so, we would be lying in our beds twenty-four hours a day in order to prevent anything bad from happening to us. But we rise up every morning and catch the train or take our cars; we go to the airport and we board a plane, and we do all these things in the assurance that we will end up in the place that we are planning to go to.

Every human being has natural faith, otherwise nobody would move, and nobody would take any action. However, this is not the kind of faith that we need. We need God's own faith. We need to have trust in God's character and in His person. We need the faith that has been born of God in our hearts through the Holy Spirit.

In Jesus' answer to Peter, He says,

"For assuredly I say to you; whoever says to this mountain 'Be removed and be cast into the sea' and does not doubt in his heart, but believes that those things he says will be done, he will have whatever he says. Therefore, I say to you whatever things you ask when you pray, believe that you receive them, and you will have them."

It is actually one of the most amazing promises we have in the New Testament concerning the power of prayer.

Jesus is promising that by the prayer of faith it will be possible to even remove mountains. He is, of course, not talking about physical mountains, and there would normally be no reason why we should try to move and relocate them. However, mountains in the Bible signify opposition and, specifically, satanic opposition, and Jesus is pointing out that for those who would intercede and pray in faith, there is a power that can remove these mountains, obstacles and hindrances and opposition that the enemy is trying to put in the way of God's people.

However, it also says the following, *"If he does not doubt in his heart, but believes that those things he says will be done, he will have whatever he says."* Now, again the major point is the heart. It is not so much what you say with your mouth, it is more what you believe in your heart.

Many years ago, a small booklet was sent to me by some friends in America with a very interesting title, namely "There is a Miracle in Your Mouth". As I was reading this little book, I understood that the author was basing his assumption upon this scripture, among others, that it is possible by confession to make things work and happen in the spiritual realm. There is no doubt that there is a great truth in having the right confession, but certainly the miracle could never be in your mouth. The miracle has to happen in your heart, because as the Lord Jesus says here, if you do not doubt in your heart, but believe, then you can say to the mountain, be lifted up and be cast into the sea. What really counts is what is in your heart; not what is in your mouth. If you do not have that faith given by the Holy Spirit in your heart, you cannot accomplish anything by just opening your mouth and issuing lots of proclamations and confessions. It is not the technique; it is not saying words that causes things to happen. That would be pure magic. It is what is in your hearts that dictates what can happen when you are confessing things.

This same principle is found in Romans 10, where Paul says

"If in your heart you believe that Jesus was raised from the dead, and with your mouth confess that He is Lord, then you shall be saved."

Notice the combination here, and even the sequence of things. First, you must believe in your heart that the Lord Jesus was raised from the dead. Then, you must confess with your mouth that He is Lord, and only then, you will experience the miracle of being saved. But if anybody tells you that you can be saved by just opening your mouth and uttering the words, "Jesus is Lord", then they are trying to fool you. You cannot be saved through a confession. You are saved through faith, and that faith has to somehow be given as a seed in your heart. Only then can you stand up and confess, and the miracle will be complete.

I am not saying that confessions are not powerful, and needful. They are, but only provided something is moving in your heart; that you are trusting the Lord in your heart.

We find the very same truth being underlined by the Lord Jesus, when in Luke's gospel 11, He teaches on the Lord's Prayer, and in the aftermath of the actual quotation of that prayer, he goes on to say in verses 11–13,

"If a son asks for bread from any father among you, will he give him a stone? Of if he asks for a fish, will he give him a serpent instead of a fish? Or if he asks for an egg, will he offer

him a scorpion? If then you being evil know how to give good gifts to your children, how much more will your heavenly Father give the Holy Spirit to those who ask Him."

The emphasis in these verses is again upon trusting in the character of our Father. We who are earthly fathers know that even if we are evil and sinful, we would never treat our children in such a way that when our son asked for bread, we would give him a stone. That would be unthinkable, and so the Lord Jesus says that if this is true about us earthly fathers who are evil, how much more will our heavenly Father give the Holy Spirit to those who ask Him. You see, it is a matter of trusting in the character of God. That is the key to successful prayer and intercession.

If an earthly father can be trusted when it comes to giving gifts to his children, how much more can we trust that our Father would only give us good things in answer to our prayers. In this matter of asking for the Holy Spirit, the essential thing is this; whether by faith we trust that our heavenly Father will give us the Holy Spirit when we ask Him.

Some years ago, I met a sister who for eleven years had been seeking the charismatic experience; the baptism of the Holy Spirit. She consulted me because she was rather distressed by the fact that God never seemed to be willing to respond to her prayers and to give her this gift of the Holy Spirit. She expressed great surprise that she as a mature and older woman of God had so much difficulty in receiving the power of the Spirit when around her in our meetings, people who were only just saved, seemed to be able to receive that gift almost automatically. And she raised the question of whether God had some particular things against her since He would not give her that experience.

Of course, I was able to assure her that God in no way wanted to mistreat her or make a difference between her and other people. But I then asked her what she really was expecting in her heart when she came before the Lord to ask Him for the baptism of the Holy Spirit, and she responded very quickly that she certainly did not expect to receive the Holy Spirit in the way "these Pentecostals" seemed to receive Him. By her reply I felt quite sure about the reason why this sister had not been able to receive the promise of the Holy Spirit. She was mistrusting God, and she was actually fearing that when praying for the Holy Spirit, God would give her something bad. When we have that kind of suspicious, fearful and unbelieving heart, we will never be able to receive anything in prayer from the Lord.

"When evil fathers are able to give good things to their children, how much more will our Father in Heaven give the Holy Spirit to those who ask Him." The question is whether we dare trust that God is our Father, and that He is entirely trustworthy, and that He would never ever give us anything wrong when we ask Him.

It is in James 5 that we find how important faith is to the whole life of prayer. In verse 17, the Apostle speaks about Elijah; that he was a man with a nature like ours, and he prayed earnestly that it would not rain, and it did not rain on the land for three years and six months. And he prayed again, and the heaven gave rain and the earth produced its fruit. Right before that statement about Elijah, James says, *"The effective, fervent prayer of a righteous man avails much."*

It is interesting that James is emphasizing that Elijah was just an ordinary man with a nature like ours, and yet he was able in prayer to influence the whole of his country to the extent that it did not rain in Israel for three years and six months, and then once again by his prayer, to make it rain again.

This is an amazing thing which we need to take to our hearts. If Elijah was able to enter into such a position before God, then we can do it also. He was living in the Old Testament where people were much more limited in their ways with God, and yet there is so much unbelief in our hearts that we would never dare to compare ourselves with a man like Elijah; and we would certainly never dream of being able to influence our nation with our prayer-life. And yet, that is exactly what Elijah did, and James stresses that we have the same possibilities as he did in this realm of prayer.

The Apostle James appears as a very plain and straight-forward person who says things the way they are. In the fifth chapter, verses 13–16, we read,

"Is anybody among you suffering, let him pray. Is anyone

cheerful, let him sing psalms. Is anyone among you sick, let him call for the elders of the Church, and let them pray over him, anointing him with oil in the name of the Lord. And the prayer of faith will save the sick and the Lord will raise him up, and if he has committed sins, he will be forgiven. Confess your trespasses to one another and pray for one another that you may be healed. The effective, fervent prayer of a righteous man avails much."

James seems to give us answers from God in these verses to any category of people in the local church. "If anybody is suffering," he says to begin with, "let him pray." This is actually a very simple, and yet most revolutionary answer. When people are going through suffering, hardships and testings, their reaction would often be to seek counsel with the pastor and the elders.

There is nothing wrong with that, but if only they knew how to pray they would be able to come through all their suffering by communicating directly with the Lord. And in this way, they would certainly ease the burden on the leadership of the local church. Also, they would experience personal growth in their spiritual lives in a much quicker and stronger way. We are not meant to lean so heavily upon mediators in our relationship with the Lord. This is actually an Old Testament concept. In the New Testament, God has, as truly as we are born again each and every one, given us access to come before His throne and to ask and pray our situation through.

Then, there is another category of people in the church; those who are cheerful. James says they should sing psalms, which means that if people are feeling well and in a good mood, and things are going well, they should not forget to turn it all into worship and thanksgiving. Because thanksgiving and worship is a way of assuring your well-being in the Lord and keeping your heart lifted and your spirit cheerful. God does not want us to be happy for the sake of being happy. God wants us to be happy for the sake of bringing glory to His name, and to become a testimony of His great faithfulness.

The third category James deals with in these verses are those who are sick. Again, his answer seems very simple: if anyone among you is sick, let him call the elders of the church, and they shall pray the prayer of faith anointing him with oil in the name of the Lord, and the sick will be saved and the Lord will raise him up. However, what often happens in the church today when someone is sick is that he will try to find some person with a special gift of healing.

He might even try to go a long distance to visit with some of the so-called "faith-healers", and I am not saying that all this couldn't be a help and am not excluding that God has given special gifts to certain individuals in the church for the blessing of the church. I am only saying that the normal way when people are sick in the church is that they should trust the Lord and follow this very simple procedure of letting the elders pray for them after having anointed them with oil. And then the Lord promises that the sick shall be saved, and the Lord will raise them up.

The great problem in all this is the lack of faith in our hearts in this ordinance, and so, whenever people are confronted with this possibility; to be prayed for by their own, well-known elders, they seem to hesitate because they know these elders so very well. They know they are weak people and that they might not be gifted in any special area, and so, they have no expectation that God will move on their behalf through their prayers. That attitude is so well-known and is again a clear manifestation of this spirit of unbelief that dwells in the hearts of God's people.

In reality, it has nothing to do with the elders whether a sick person will be healed or not. The elders are only instrumental in this process. It is not even the oil that is poured out upon the sick that in some magical way causes healing to come. It is a matter of faith; whether there is faith in the heart of the sick person, and in the hearts of the local elders. When there is faith, there is a great breakthrough in the realm of prayer. If there is no faith, everything becomes a ceremonial tradition and a religious habit in the Church, which will not bring anything along with it.

It has been said about the well known Chinese Bible teacher, Watchman Nee, that the Lord many years ago, in the earlier years of his ministry, taught him this lesson of trusting in the Lord and in the simple ordinances of the Word of God. Brother Nee had a weak bodily constitution and was very often sick during his many travels to spread the gospel across China. As he was so often sick, he would, however, also very often experience the Lord's sovereign touch when he turned to him in prayer. But when the Lord wanted to show brother Nee the principle of the church, he was allowed to experience a very special happening.

On one of his journeys, he came to a small village where he was supposed to have a meeting with the local believers. However, as he arrived there, he fell sick and had to stay in bed. And as he was lying there, he cried out to the Lord for His touch once again, to heal him and raise him up so that he could be ready for ministry when the people came to the house for the evening service. But this time the Lord clearly answered his request by this word, "If anyone among you is sick, let him call the elders of the church."

Brother Nee was very surprised and replied to the Lord that the Lord had so many times directly intervened to heal him so why should he then bother to call the elders. But as he kept on praying and renewing his request for healing, the same word would come back to him, "If anyone among you is sick, let him call the elders of the church."

In the course of his prayers, Brother Nee complained to the Lord that these elders were actually newly saved and all of them were illiterate; they were poor, illiterate fishermen, and so nothing special could be expected of them in terms of praying for his healing. But the Lord replied by the same word, "If anyone among you is sick, let him call the elders of the church."

So, finally, Brother Nee sent for the elders, who came after work into the bedroom, still stinking from the smell of fish, and Brother Nee brought before them his request to be prayed for and anointed with oil according to James 5. However, then the leading elder said, "Well, we cannot read, so we don't know exactly what is written in James 5. Would you please read it out loud for us," and so Brother Nee read the text, and upon discovering that he needed oil, the leading brother turned to the wife of the house and asked, "Do you have any oil in the house?", and she said, "Yes, but I am afraid it is only fish oil." The leading elder was satisfied with this and said, "oil is oil," and so she brought out a big bottle of fish oil.

However, since these elders were not familiar with the later traditions of the church, the leading elder opened the bottle and poured the oil on Brother Nee in his bed, and it was said that Brother Nee was stinking from fish oil for several weeks after this experience.

After he was anointed with oil, they put their hands upon him and prayed and then left the place. And quickly thereafter, the Lord touched Brother Nee, and he stood up and he was completely healed and was able to continue with his ministry.

This is an example of what we are talking about. *"Do not cast away your confidence because it has a great reward."* It is not a matter of learning how to intercede and how to pray and how to formulate the prayers so that they might impress the good Lord in heaven. It is a matter of what is in our hearts, and if we are going to see and break through in intercession, we need to confess our unbelieving hearts before God and be cleansed and purified from this spirit of unbelief so that we very simply can once again come back to trusting in the character of God, and in the truth and in the purity of His own word.

Power Tools for Prayer

In the New Testament, there are five different types of prayer mentioned. Four of them we find in 1 Timothy 2:1, where Paul is saying,

"Therefore, I exhort first of all that supplications, prayers, intercessions and giving of thanks be made for all men."

The fifth one is found in Ephesians 6 and is what we understand as spiritual warfare, or even better: prayer warfare.

The purpose of this booklet is not to deal with spiritual warfare, and so we will not go into much detail on this fifth category. However, I do feel prompted to say in this connection that the term "spiritual warfare" in my understanding is not a very good choice. The term "spiritual warfare" has its actual origin in the occult movements where they have been practising their kind of spiritual warfare for decades, which is bringing people together and issuing curses primarily against the Church and Christian leaders. I would much prefer the term "prayer warfare" because generally speaking, "spiritual warfare" is only found in the context of prayer in the New Testament.

There is no such thing as direct confrontation with the powers of darkness except through the ministry of prayer. And prayer always means that we focus on the Lord and that we appeal to the Lord, and that even our warfare against the powers of darkness goes through the Lord and has to come before the throne. And so, in a way, we are not the ones doing the warfare, the Lord is the one who is coming against the enemy in response to our prayers.

The whole chapter of Ephesians 6 shows us clearly that the spiritual conflict that the Church is experiencing with the powers of darkness and the operation of the whole armour of God is something that is only workable in the situation of prayer. That is why the term "prayer warfare" is a much more accurate description to signify the nature of the spiritual battle that we are in.

In 1 Timothy 2:1, Paul mentions four different kinds of prayer that are available for the Church. And let me first of all underline that it is essential that we receive all the things that God has for us and never become one-sided. In modern times, there has been a tendency since the discovery of spiritual warfare to only major on that aspect of the prayer ministry, trying to think that we are able to solve all the problems by just cutting off the enemy. This is far from being true, and when the scriptures mention five different disciplines of prayer, we, of course, need to practise all five in order to be complete in our intercessory ministry.

1. Supplications

The first type of prayer mentioned by Paul is "supplications". "Supplications" simply mean calling upon the Lord. They do not necessarily describe a very eloquent type of utterance in prayer; they do not even imply that those who are doing supplications necessarily have the full understanding of the situation for which they are praying, or the perfect understanding of God's will. It is simply the outcry of the heart of the people because they are in a desperate situation of need.

Many modern theologians do not believe that there is a need for this kind of prayer. They tend to believe that we are able to fulfil everything through proclamations of faith and proclamations of spiritual warfare. However, this is far from being right. Supplications are perhaps the most powerful type of prayer found in the whole Bible. It is certainly that form of prayer which impresses the heart of God the Father most.

It was supplications that actually delivered the people of Israel from their situation of bondage in Egypt. We remember how Pharaoh through his slave masters terrorized and tyrannized God's people in Egypt more and more until it became quite unbearable, and the people began to cry to the Lord, and in Exodus 2:23–25,

"Now it happened in the process of time that the king of Egypt died. Then the children of Israel groaned because of the bondage, and they cried out; and their cry came up to God because of the bondage. So, God heard their groaning, and God remembered His covenant with Abraham, with Isaac and with Jacob. And God looked upon the children of Israel and God acknowledged them."

It was this tremendous cry for mercy that came out of the hearts of the Israelites that made God remember His covenant with Abraham, Isaac, and Jacob, and it was out of that strong supplication that God took action and called Moses at the burning bush in the wilderness and sent him to Egypt to deliver God's people from their affliction.

This is how strong supplications are in prayer, and in every kind of revival we have seen in the history of the Church, supplication has played a very significant role. So, as we as God's people learn to just open our hearts and cry out to God because of the need that we are in, first of all within the Church, but also within our nation, we will be able to touch His heart in a very special way.

We must never forget that God primarily sees Himself as our Father. And as a father, He has a very tender heart, and the strongest part of God's character is that of mercy. He is a holy God, He is a righteous God, He is a faithful God, but beyond all these other qualities, He is a God of mercy, and that is our great opportunity when we think about the situation we are in, within the Church and within the nation. We can actually call upon the name of the Lord.

We can appeal to His mercy, and even if we are still in rebellion, and even if we are still a stiff-necked people, who certainly do not deserve any salvation, or any deliverance, or any revival, God will be touched when His people are crying out their hearts before Him. And He will respond and pour out His grace and His mercy upon the whole situation.

There is great power in supplications. Also, in the New Testament, we find that type of prayer spoken of. In Romans 10:11–13, it says,

"The Scripture says, that whoever believes on Him will not be put to shame, for there is no distinction between Jew and Greek. For the same Lord over all is rich to all who call upon Him. For whoever calls on the name of the Lord shall be saved."

This is truly the way to salvation. Whoever calls on the name of the Lord shall be saved. Maybe you remember your own conversion; how much did you know about the Lord; about His law; about principles of Christian living? Most of us did not even know God, let alone His Word or His statutes, but because we were in deep need and desperate because of our sins, we opened our hearts and we called upon the name of the Lord. And what happened? We were saved. What a tremendous power there is in supplication, from both the individual as well as from God's people.

It is my understanding that supplications are the most powerful factor in producing a revival. This is actually the type of prayer that is dominant among God's people when revival comes, because it is the very same principle as with the people of Israel in Egypt. Once we reach the point where we are no longer able to tolerate what is going on, and we are, as it were, fed up with our own deadness, with the deadness of the Church, and the abundance of sin among the people in the midst of whom we live, we will also begin to call upon the name of the Lord and cry out our desperate need to Heaven, and that will make the Lord respond with great power.

So, there is a great need for this quality of prayer in the

ministry of intercession today.

2. Prayers of Petition

The second type of prayer is called "prayers of petition". They refer to the concrete way in which God wants us to put our requests before Him. So much prayer in the Church has developed into religious talk-shows, where we are just telling the Lord stories or quoting scriptures, or just airing our different theological views instead of really asking the Lord for specific things. After all, prayer means that we ask for specific things and God gives us specific things.

If you go to a church today and you attend the prayer meeting, you will find very little real prayer going on. As I said before, because of a lack of faith, the level of prayer has sunk down into becoming a religious performance, where we use our time to exhibit our own spirituality in prayer. You know the people who, when they pray, are basically just walking across the whole globe and asking God for this and that, and the other, without really having anything specific burning in their hearts. You know the people who take up the time of our prayer meetings to make Bible expositions and deliver good Bible studies to all those who are present, without any specific request to be made before the Lord.

God wants us to know that prayer is asking of Him specific things, and expecting Him to give us what we pray about.

I once made an experiment in my church at a time when the Lord was teaching me the nature of real prayer. As the pastor, I was often standing in the door-way to greet people when they left the church after a meeting. But this particular evening, I had upon my heart to ask each and every brother and sister who participated in the prayer meeting to tell me what they had specifically asked the Lord for that night. It was a shocking experience, and I am not sure that I would ever like to repeat it. Most of the people did not even have a clue as to what they had asked God for that evening, other people were so confused about the whole prayer meeting that they did not have any sense of direction.

That evening taught me a very important lesson; that God will not have us use our prayer meetings to make religious talk-shows, but He wants us to learn what petitions are all about; to come before His face and to ask specific things of Him. After all, this is what the Lord Jesus taught us, *"If you ask about anything you want, it shall be given unto you by My Father who is in heaven."* Jesus is talking about specific things, and that is what God delights to hear from His children.

We have to make sure when entering the process of prayer that we know what we really want from God, both in our own individual lives, and also when we are interceding for the Church, and also, actually, when we are seeking God for our nation. We must be able to tell the Lord that we want the Lord to do this and that and the other. That is the discipline of petitions, or requests in the life of prayer.

3. Intercessions

Intercessions is the third type of prayer mentioned in 1 Timothy 2:1 and since this is the overall subject of this little booklet, we have already gone into some of the differences between ordinary prayer and intercession.

At this point, I would like to underline that intercession is a deeper form of prayer. We have already seen that it requires a much stronger commitment. Ordinary prayer can be offered up for people and situations at a distance, so to speak, but if we desire to enter into intercession, we need to know how to identify with those for whom we are interceding. Identification is perhaps the most basic difference between ordinary prayer and intercession. We can all offer up prayers for people and situations every day, while that kind of practice does not really affect our own personal situation. But as soon as we talk about intercession, this is no longer enough. We cannot remain in our own secure position.

We need to move from where we are and to take the place of the people for whom we are interceding. We need to know what it means to identify with those who are in deep trouble, and deep need. The true mark of intercessory prayer is that we have taken upon ourselves the burdens that belong to those for whom we are praying.

Rees Howells, the great intercessor from Wales was a remarkable man in this respect. In the biography called "The Intercessor", it speaks about the way Rees Howells identified with some of the people for whom he was praying. In the particular city where he was living, there was a very wild person, a vagabond and an alcoholic, a man of violence who was known in the city for his very bad behaviour. He would also visit the churches and disrupt and destroy the services and work there, and so the believers in the city were deeply concerned for this man, and were spending much time in prayer for him.

Rees Howells was among those who were praying for this man, when the Holy Spirit put upon his heart a special burden to intercede for this troubled person. As soon as Rees Howells started praying for this man, the Holy Spirit impressed upon his heart that he needed to identify with this man's desperate situation, and he needed to do it in a very physical way. This man was living in the slum; he was addicted to alcohol; he never washed himself; and he was growing an unending beard. And the Spirit said to Rees Howells that he should go and live together with this man for some time in order to get the feel of this man's need and also to show this man the love of God.

So, he left his nice secure home and although he, of course, did not identify in the matter of drinking or hygiene, he decided to stay in the same place as this poor man and thereby identify with his situation, while crying out to the Lord on his behalf.

After some time, the burden upon Rees Howell's life for this man's salvation became so strong that he started feeling that if God would not save this sinner, he would never be able to be released from his commitment and return to his home. He actually felt the burden so strongly upon himself as if it had really become a matter of his own life or death. And it was when he came to that point that the Lord gave heed to his prayers and sovereignly and miraculously met this violent drunkard and saved and delivered him and made him a great testimony in the city.

This is the true heart of intercession. We need to remember how the Lord Jesus did exactly that. Jesus could have stayed in glory and He could have offered up the most beautiful, eloquent and righteous prayers for our salvation, but in His love the Son of God left His glory and came down to identify completely with our sorrows, our sins and with our human life. In all details he was tempted, in everything but without sin, and it was in that position that Jesus was able to intercede for us and to work out our salvation.

When some years ago, the Lord put upon my heart to pray especially for the Jewish people to be released from the Communist Soviet Union, I felt after a while that I needed to go and see how the Jewish people were living in the former Soviet Union. So, I joined up with a team on a prayer tour to some of the major, Jewish communities there, and it was on that trip that I began to realize what it means to intercede for a group of people.

As we met some of the Jews in Moscow, and in Odessa and other places, and we sensed the great danger and oppression and persecution they were living under, it became quite another thing to pray for their release than if we had just stayed at home in our own countries and offered up prayers on their behalf.

I remember, especially, in the city of Volgograd how the Lord put us in touch with a Jewish man, who brought us to his brother and sister-in-law, who were living in a flat in a city. As we were able to share with them about Israel and about the coming-home of the Jewish people from all the four corners of the earth to their ancient land of their forefathers, they were so taken by that prospect that we had to spend several hours extra explaining everything to them.

As we left their flat, I remember how as we were sitting in the car to be taken back to the hotel, the Jewish man came running down the stairs, opened the back door of the car where I was sitting, and with tears running down his face, said with a heart full of desire, "Please come back and help us to return to Israel."

I remember how I began to cry as well, and when I returned from the Soviet Union and was praying for the Jewish people over there to be released, I could picture this tearful face as if in a vision, and I could hear that voice begging, "Come back and help us to get out of here." That made such a difference to my way of praying, and my commitment to pray for the Jews to be released from the Soviet Union.

Because this is what intercession is about; to identify with people in their need and to share their burden, and to a certain extent, feel some of their pain and distress upon our own lives.

When we speak about identification, we need to be aware of the fact that we cannot carry this principle too far. There are Christians who tend to believe that we might be able to confess other people's sins in such a way that God would save these people. That is not so and this cannot be found in the Word of God. It is true that we are able to repent on behalf of the sins of other people and to plead with God for mercy and grace, but it cannot replace the confessions and the repentance of these people for their own salvation. What it can do is to open up the way for more grace and more mercy and it can buy these sinners more time so that they might eventually turn to God. But it cannot replace their own asking for forgiveness personally. This is never possible.

We do know that Daniel identified with the people of Israel and he confessed his sins and the sins of his people, and by doing so he influenced the heart of God to have mercy and show grace with the people of Israel in the Babylonian captivity, and to release them and lead them back to the land of Israel.

We also know that Moses identified with the people of Israel in their rebellion against God, and he confessed sins on their behalf, and he asked for mercy and the Lord gave extra grace so as to not destroy the people, but to give them extended opportunities to turn away from their wicked ways and repent of their sins.

Our identification cannot replace people's personal responsibility for their sins, but it can give them extra favour with God, and extra mercy, and long-suffering.

In the same way, when we are standing in the gap for our nation and repenting on behalf of the wickedness and the sins of our people, we do not imagine that God would take that as a substitute for repentance among our people and, so to speak, save our whole people in one go. This is not possible. What we are doing is asking God for a visitation; we are asking God to send a revival in His grace instead of putting judgement upon our people with the destruction that follows. Such an identification has great power with God and touches His heart, and as with Moses when he interceded for Israel, God promised to delay the account that had to be made over the sins of the people and to give them extra opportunity to turn away from their rebellion and turn back to the Lord.

4. Giving of Thanks

The fourth type of prayer mentioned here is "giving of thanks". This is, of course, a part of worship, and worship plays an important role in intercession. But as it is expressed here, it has a very special meaning.

Thanksgiving is the evidence of having faith in the Lord. No matter where we turn in the New Testament, we will always find that giving of thanks has its place. This is because giving of thanks is an evidence of honouring and glorifying God as God in each and every situation. When we intercede for very grave problems, and even when we supplicate before God for the dreadful situation we see in our nation, we must always remember that God is altogether righteous. It has never been God's fault and never will be, that things are the way they are. And so, in our intercession, we need to remember to give God His place of supremacy and to honour His name and to, as it were, keep Him free of any blame for whatever may be going on.

Thanksgiving is in this way a powerful type of prayer that enables the Lord to respond to our prayers with favour and with pleasure. There is actually no situation in which we ought not lift up the holy name of God and thank Him for being the wonderful Father that He is.

The Purpose of Intercession

When we talk about intercession and why the Lord is calling us to exercise this tremendously important ministry, we need to understand what the real purpose is.

To pray for the sake of just exercising a religious habit is quite meaningless. Also, it makes very little sense to separate the ministry of intercession from the overall purposes of God. Intercessors are not supposed to become a special group of people who are only concentrating on prayer. We are to see ourselves as a part of what God is doing in an overall sense, and we also have to line ourselves up with other ministries in the Body of Christ.

The overall purpose of the work of the Church is to bring in the Kingdom of God. We do not pray because it has some kind of personal satisfaction, we pray in order to prosper God's purposes on earth.

One of the clearest goals we find in the Bible for intercessory prayer is to produce a spiritual revival in the society in which we live. This is also the great motivation behind Paul's exhortation in 1 Timothy 2 when he is exhorting us to pray for all men and for kings and all who are in authority. He is doing so in view of the desperate need for a spiritual revival to be brought about in our society.

The prayer-ministry of the Church has a very positive focus. Its purpose is not in the first hand to battle against the negative things and against sin in the world, but to open up the way for an outpouring of the Holy Spirit that will revive the Church and that will bring multitudes of people into the Kingdom of God.

In 1 Timothy 2, the Apostle Paul is giving the Church an assignment to pray these different kinds of prayer for all men, and for kings and for all who are in authority. Notice that Paul begins by saying that he exhorts us *"first of all."* He is listing a clear first priority in the work of the Church.

The letters to his young friend and co-worker Timothy are letters of instruction to the local church for its work and its service, and as we read through these two letters we find a number of different important subjects, such as men and women in the church; the qualifications for the ministry of being elders and deacons; warnings against the coming of a great apostasy; the care for widows and ministry towards the poor and needy.

All in all, we are talking about a number of important

instructions for the local congregation, but the very first on the list – and this is important – deals with the prayer ministry of the Church. Paul is actually exhorting the Church to exercise these four different kinds of prayer as the first and most important ministry of the local church.

And yet, it appears that this first commandment is not being obeyed. However, it does not really matter what else the Church might be doing, the first call for the local church in ministry is to pray. And especially to pray for all men who are living in the local society, and for kings and those in authority, not just for the local affairs of the church.

If the church had really taken this exhortation to heart and practised it as its first priority on a regular basis, I am convinced that the situation in our nations would look much different to what it does today. Basically, the Church of Jesus Christ has forgotten this instruction, and whereas we have been eager to work in evangelism, in social work, and to build our church organizations, we have totally forgotten the first and most important calling; to be a Body of prayer for revival in our local society.

I am in no way implying that evangelism is not important, or that social work and mercy ministries do not have their place, or even that it is not essential to pray for the Church, I am only trying to put our priorities right. The first thing that Paul is sharing with Timothy to be practised in all the churches of the Early Church, is the fourfold ministry of prayer.

We are called, then, to intercede for all men. That means many more people than those who happen to belong to the Church. The vast majority of men are still outside the Church. How shall we understand this calling? It cannot possibly be that Paul wants the local church to, as it were, embrace the whole world in its prayers. When we add to this exhortation the calling to pray for kings and all who are in authority, we are entitled to understand this calling *"to pray for all men"* as praying for all those who are part of the society in which we live.

In a narrower sense, it means to pray for our city, and in a broader sense, it means to pray for the nation under whose rule we are living. It is not always easy to know how to practise praying even for all men who live in our society, but there are some churches who have found a good and systematic way to fulfil and to obey this calling.

I know of a church that has divided the people of the city up into the different classes in society and then has allotted prayer assignments to different prayer groups in the church. There is one group that especially prays for the city government, the mayor and the city senate. Another group has been assigned the working class, and yet another one is praying for the children and the schools. Yet another one is responsible to especially intercede for the poor people and the drug addicts, and so on. When the church meets for prayer once a week, they spend about six hours together praying in groups for all these different classes of people within their city.

The amazing thing has been that because of their intercession, the prayer groups of this church have become involved in communicating with the particular groups of people that they are praying for. And they have had the joy of even seeing close contacts being established on a regular basis, for example to the city authorities. Also, they have seen several people being saved through their work of intercessory prayer.

Why is it so important for the Apostle Paul to underline the necessity of praying for kings and all who are in authority? Many Christians draw back, as it were, as soon as they hear talk about praying for governments and people in authority, because they instinctively feel that we are trying to deal with politics. But that is far from being the case. I do not believe that God is calling us to support any particular party politics, but the scripture clearly reveals that the government as an institution is something that has been established by God for the sake of the people's lives and their security.

We have to admit that people in government do have an influence on those that they are ruling over in quite an extensive way, and so, it makes a difference whether we have people of a righteous standing leading our cities and our nations or if those who are in the place of authority are given to corruption and to abuse of power.

Secondly, prayers for those in authority has much more to do with the unseen powers behind the physical government. We know that this present world is in the hands of the evil one, and that the devil has established his structure of rulership over nations and cities, and that he has established principalities and powers to rule on his behalf over local areas and regions, and over nations. When the Church does not intercede for the government, it gives the powers of darkness an opportunity to influence the government. And this is what we have seen so clearly in experience over the past many years.

Today, there is hardly any government in the Western world, or any nation, that is not deeply infiltrated by the powers of darkness. We have, for instance, in several European governments, cabinet members who are members of the Freemasons or other occult movements under the New Age. No wonder the continent of Europe is getting farther and farther away from its original Christian basis. The devil seems to have gained a foothold into the government seats of so many nations in the world, which is by and large because the Church is not fulfilling its role to cut off the powers of darkness from influencing the human governments, and replacing the powers of darkness with the influence of the Holy Spirit.

It is the Church in prayer that makes the difference, and that is the reason why Paul is calling for the Church to pray for kings and those in authority in order, as he goes on to point out that

"we may lead a quiet and peaceable life in all godliness and reverence for this is good and acceptable in the sight of God our Saviour."

Paul is here speaking about peace and righteousness and reverence in the human society. He is not necessarily talking about a Christian, or a saved community, but he is talking about a spirit of righteousness prevailing even in the secular society. It is important for us to know that intercession has the power to change the spiritual climate in a nation and in a city, and to cut off the influence of the powers of darkness and bring about a sense of righteousness in the hearts of the rulers as well as in the hearts of the people.

That is one aspect of revival. Revival is more than people entering into the Kingdom of God. It is that as well, because in all revivals, there has been a great harvest of unsaved people who have entered into the Kingdom of God. But there has been more than that; there has been an impact upon the whole society by the power of the Holy Spirit, and that is what Paul is pointing out here in 1 Timothy 2. When the Church is obeying the calling to intercede for the secular society, and for those who are in government, there will be a change in the spiritual climate. A spirit of unrighteousness and corruption and abuse of power will be replaced by a spirit of righteousness.

Another reason for Paul's exhortation for the Church to intercede is clearly to open up a way for the gospel to be received in secular society. He goes on to say that

"God our Saviour desires all men to be saved and to come to the knowledge of the truth, for there is one God and one Mediator between God and men, the Man, Christ Jesus who gave Himself a ransom for all to be testified in due time."

Paul is here pointing out that the prayer ministry of the Church will be to open up a way for the gospel to be preached and to be received by people in secular society.

So often, in evangelism, we tend to forget that we need more than good and anointed preaching of the gospel. We also need people who are listening to be delivered from satanic oppression and deception, and to have their hearts prepared and opened to receive the Word of Truth. Intercession is able to bring that about in the hearts of people in the community in which we live. Therefore, we see that whenever the Church is moving in prayer there will be a thirst and hunger created in the unsaved people, and there will be a seeking of God from sinners everywhere in the city in which we live.

Paul concludes as follows, *"I desire therefore that men pray everywhere, lifting up holy hands without wrath and doubting."*

What Paul is aiming at here is that in every locality, in every geographical place, there will be a prayer ministry in the Body of Christ of men and women who are lifting up holy hands without wrath and doubting. This is God's greatest desire today. When we are thinking about promoting the Kingdom of God in our area, we are so often thinking about doing evangelism and planting churches in the first place, but Paul's concept is different.

Paul sees prayer groups being established in all areas as the first step; groups of men and women who are moving in unity and who have settled their differences and have put their relationships right so that they can pray without doubt and without wrath, such groups lifting up holy hands before God to exercise intercession; this is the first step to conquer an area for the Kingdom of God.

May the Lord in His mercy help us to understand this priority in God's heart for the work of the Church. There is no doubt in my mind whatsoever that intercession is the most powerful ministry that the Church of Jesus Christ today can exercise, and that it is also the most needed ministry to bring about a breakthrough for the gospel in the cities and the nations of the world. There is, therefore, every reason for us to come to learn the secrets and the principles of true intercession.

If you have enjoyed this book and would like to help us to send a copy of it and many other titles to needy pastors in the **Third World**, please write for further information or send your gift to:

Sovereign World Trust, P.O. Box 777, Tonbridge, Kent TN11 9XT, United Kingdom

or to the **'Sovereign World'** distributor in your country. If sending money from outside the United Kingdom, please send an International Money Order or Foreign Bank Draft in STERLING, drawn on a **UK** bank to **Sovereign World Trust**.